The Locomotives of
SIR NIGEL
GRESLEY

Patrick Stephens Limited, a member of the Haynes Publishing Group, has published authoritative, quality books for enthusiasts for more than 20 years. During that time the company has established a reputation as one of the world's leading publishers of books on aviation, maritime, military, model-making, motor cycling, motoring, motor racing, railway and railway modelling subjects. Readers or authors with suggestions for books they would like to see published are invited to write to: The Editorial Director, Patrick Stephens Limited, Sparkford, Nr Yeovil, Somerset BA22 7JJ.

The Locomotives of SIR NIGEL GRESLEY

by

O.S. Nock

New Edition

With a Foreword by

O.V. Bulleid

Chief Mechanical Engineer, Southern Railway

Patrick Stephens Limited

© O.S. Nock 1945 and 1991

First published by Longmans, Green & Co Ltd in 1945, compiled from articles appearing in *The Railway Magazine* in 1941-3. Second expanded and re-illustrated edition published by Patrick Stephens Limited in 1991.

British Library Cataloguing in Publication Data
Nock, O.S. (Oswald Stevens) 1905-
The locomotives of Sir Nigel Gresley.—2nd. ed.
1. Great Britain. Steam locomotives designed by Gresley, Nigel
I. Title
625.261092

ISBN 1-85260-336-4

Patrick Stephens Limited is a member of the Haynes Publishing Group P.L.C., Sparkford, Nr Yeovil, Somerset BA22 7JJ.

Typesetting by MJL Limited, Hitchin, Hertfordshire.
Printed in Great Britain

1 3 5 7 9 10 8 6 4 2

Contents

Sir Herbert Nigel Gresley CBE DSc MInstCE MIMechE MIEE MInstT
Locomotive Engineer, GNR, 1911-22
Chief Mechanical Engineer, LNER, 1923-41
(*British Railways*)

Foreword

to the original edition
by O.V. Bulleid

This book is a comprehensive review of the work of the most notable English locomotive engineer of his generation.

The reader will be interested in the many excellent photographs, diagrams, and tables and will obtain a clear picture of the growth in power and sustained capacity of the steam locomotive over the thirty years from 1911 to 1941.

The adaptability of the steam locomotive to changing operating conditions and demands is brought out, examples being the performances of *Papyrus* in March 1935, and *Trigo* and *Singapore* in March 1939.

Sir Nigel Gresley was more than the Locomotive Engineer of one company. His constant search for improvements, his awareness of developments in all locomotive engineering, and his interest in all advances in engineering practice in fields however remotely related to railway work, were reflected in the adaptation to his locomotives of the work of other engineers.

The book therefore enables the development of the locomotive to be followed in all its phases.

The descriptions of the original design, as for example of the first 4-6-2 type engine, and the subsequent improvements incorporated in it to meet more difficult conditions, will be followed with care. The improvements made in a basically sound design and the substantially better performance made possible are instanced in the Ivatt Atlantics.

The locomotive designer will find much information of assistance to him; he will read with value the alterations made in valve gear settings, and the effect they had on the working of the engine; he will note the care taken to design the locomotive to suit the operating conditions.

All locomotive men will thank Mr Nock for producing so enjoyable and instructive an account of the locomotives of Sir Nigel Gresley.

COAT OF ARMS
LONDON AND NORTH EASTERN RAILWAY.

Author's Preface to the original edition

This book is for the most part a reprint of a series of articles that appeared in *The Railway Magazine* between February 1941 and April 1943. In reprinting, however, opportunity has been taken to include certain items which the exigencies of wartime publication caused to be omitted from the original articles. There are also included details of a number of noteworthy locomotive performances that I have been privileged to record, from time to time, particulars of which have previously been published in the 'British Locomotive Practice and Performance' feature of *The Railway Magazine*.

At the time the original series of articles was planned, I expected it would present an unfinished story, carried only as far as the outbreak of war in 1939, and that at some future time I should be able to resume, and record still more striking developments after the end of hostilities. Sir Nigel's sudden death in April 1941, however, brought the story unexpectedly to a conclusion.

The earlier locomotive history of the Great Northern Railway has been presented and finely illustrated in Mr G.F. Bird's book*, in which the story is brought up to the end of the Ivatt régime. The present book takes up the story where the earlier one left off. In so doing, however, I have not attempted to give a complete chronicle of the locomotive building carried out under Sir Nigel Gresley's direction, nor to record the smaller variations in details that have been incorporated in successive batches of some of the larger classes. My aim has been to present a broad outline of the development of locomotive design, first on the Great Northern and then on the London & North Eastern Railway, and to let the details of actual performances on the road themselves provide evidence of the efficacy of the products of Doncaster, Darlington, Stratford and Gorton works during this period.

In so doing I must first of all acknowledge the invaluable assistance I received from Sir Nigel himself, in placing his personal albums at my disposal; from these albums many of the illustrations in this book are taken.[†] I am also particularly indebted to

---

*The Locomotives of the Great Northern Railway (pub 1903-10).

[†]This new edition has been largely re-illustrated.

Mr E.G. Marsden, through whose good offices as Information Agent of the LNER during the years 1934-9, I was afforded many privileges for observing Gresley locomotives at work; and to Messrs I.S.W. Groom and G.A. Musgrave, Locomotive Running Superintendents of the Southern and Scottish Areas respectively, for the privilege of observing many of these performances from the footplate. To Mr George Dow, Press Relations Officer of the LNER, I am also indebted for some valuable help.

In addition to these officers of the London & North Eastern Railway, I am glad to acknowledge the help I have received from many other friends whose status might seem a little puzzling to any casual reader. The term 'amateur' is too often used in a derogatory sense nowadays to be suitable; and one could certainly not call them outsiders, for several are professional railwaymen, though not serving in either the Locomotive Running, or the CMEs Department. Robert Stephenson, in availing himself of the advice and help of his two great contemporaries Locke and Brunel on the Menai Bridge Council, designated them 'friendly volunteer assistants'. This pleasant term most happily meets my case. Among these good friends I must mention particularly Mr K.A.C.R. Nunn, Driver G.H. Haygreen (retired), and Mr R.A.H. Weight; among photographers Mr Gordon Tidey and Mr E.R. Wethersett each took several pictures specially for the original series of articles; and lastly my sincere thanks are due to Mr W.J. Reynolds who put his entire collection of blocks at my disposal, thereby enabling the book to be illustrated much more lavishly than would otherwise have been possible.

During the time the original series of articles was in preparation, I was in close personal touch with the LNER, and travelling on the line frequently. Yet, through circumstances connected with the war, when the time came for publication I was living far away, in a county where even amid the complexities of wartime locomotive operating Gresley locomotives are rare visitors, and where only for one single fortnight exactly twenty years ago has it ever been possible to witness the stirring spectacle of a Gresley Pacific at speed. Thanks however to the kindness of friends in London, Newcastle, Edinburgh, Glasgow and elsewhere, I have been kept well posted as to what is happening on the LNER, and so I have been able to complete the task with all the advantage of copious eye-witness information readily at hand.

In conclusion, my warmest thanks are due to Mr Bulleid for contributing so generous a foreword to this book.

O.S. Nock
Chippenham, Wilts
May 1945

Author's Preface to the new edition

In the autumn of 1936 *The Railway Magazine* began publishing a short series of articles that I had written about the 'Locomotives of the LNWR from 1897-1922'. At that time my great friend Edward Marsden was in charge of the press section of the Chief General Manager's office on the LNER at Kings Cross, and we used to meet frequently. One day he broadly hinted that having dealt with the LNWR, what about doing something similar about the LNER? We had several talks, and I eventually decided to do something about the locomotives of Sir Nigel Gresley. *The Railway Magazine* took some persuading, and by that time the war clouds had gathered over Europe, and Marsden had been taken from the LNER to become an assistant secretary to the Railway Executive Committee. We kept in touch, however, and when at last the first instalment of 'The Locomotives of Sir Nigel Gresley' was in proof form I sent him a copy.

When it was published, in February 1941, Marsden sought an early opportunity of seeing Sir Nigel Gresley to ask him what he thought of it. The great man was apparently delighted, save that he thought there were not enough pictures! It was wartime, however, with all the attendant restrictions, but Gresley waved that aside, and immediately made arrangements for his personal albums to be sent to *The Railway Magazine*. Gresley was kind enough to read the proofs of the next few instalments, but then, in April 1941, he died, at the relatively early age of 64. The series of articles eventually ran to ten instalments, the last indeed not appearing in *The Railway Magazine* until March 1943.

By that time the depredations wrought by his successor had already begun to take effect. All true locomotive enthusiasts were incensed, but the spearhead of the attack was W.J. Reynolds, who wrote some pungent letters to *The Railway Gazette*. He was indeed a power in the land, not only Editor of the Journal of the Stephenson Locomotive Society and an expert locomotive photographer of more than 40 years' experience, but he was also a senior editor on the staff of Longmans Green, the publishers. He persuaded *The Railway Magazine* to allow Longmans to republish the articles in book form, and taking charge of the whole job personally, adding many of his own photographs, he produced in splendid form the first of my works to be so published.

Forty-five years onward, the locomotive *Sir Nigel Gresley*, having performed in distinguished style under private ownership for nearly 30 years, had been at Steamtown, Carnforth, for general overhaul, and my present publishers thought that it would be a pleasant gesture to the re-emergence of the locomotive to reprint the original book, suitably updating it to cover the work of the Gresley locomotive to the end of steam on British Railways, and with some account of the exploits of the preserved locomotives subsequently. I have therefore added three additional chapters, leaving the original ten chapters unaltered. In an Appendix I have also added a list of the Gresley engines that were named. Not all the photographs used in the original book are now available but I have been able to supplement those that are with many others from my photographer friends.

O.S. Nock
Bath
1991

1

GNR, 1911-1914

The career of Sir Nigel Gresley has no parallel in British locomotive history. First as Locomotive Superintendent of the Great Northern Railway, and then as Chief Mechanical Engineer of the LNER, his chieftainship bridges not merely 30 years of great events in the railway world, but has also witnessed a complete transition from the old operating methods, when engines were nursed and groomed like racehorses, to the stringent economic conditions of today. It links the time when single-wheelers were still being used on crack expresses to our modern streamline age, when up to the outbreak of war developments both at home and overseas were following thick and fast upon each other.

Throughout GNR and LNER history there has been a marked continuity in the locomotive design of these companies. The streamlined Pacifics are lineal descendents, not merely of the large-boilered Ivatt Atlantics, but of far older types—the Stirling 8-footers, and, even before them, the celebrated Sturrock 4-2-2, No 215. The big changes that often take place on the appointment of a new chief are absent in Great Northern history, yet each engineer, in developing the practice of his predecessor, has not been content merely to keep abreast of traffic requirements. In the early

At the start of the Gresley regime on the GNR: a Stirling 7 ft 7 in 2-2-2 rebuilt with a domed boiler, No 873, in Hadley Woods with a Cambridge express. (*C. Laundy*)

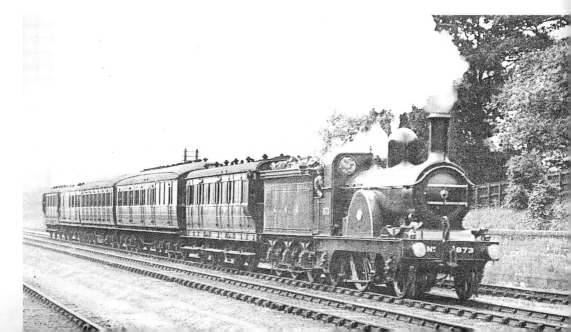

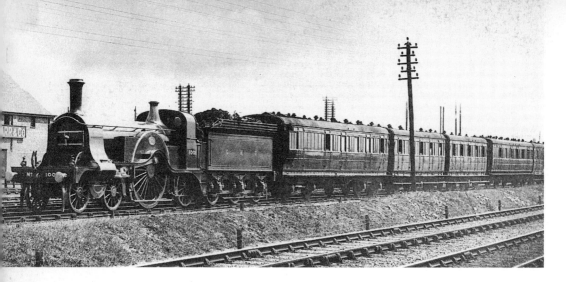

One of the last Stirling 8-foot singles, No 1001, on an East Lincolnshire express just after leaving Peterborough. (*C. Laundy*)

years of each regime an outstanding express design has been produced which with various refinements has remained the standard type for very many years.

Stirling's was the 4-2-2 era; during Ivatt's reign, although singles and 4-4-0s were regularly employed in express service, one could not regard the Great Northern as anything but a 4-4-2 line, and Sir Nigel Gresley's day is that of the Pacific. The arrival on the scene of the 4-6-2s was delayed by the last war, but the experience gained during the war in the haulage of enormous loads—by pre-1914 standards—was probably of no small value in the preparation of the Pacific design. Again although one wheel arrangement has remained standard throughout each era, the pioneer design in each case has been materially improved during the career of its creator. One would no more think of equating the merits of a non superheater 'Klondyke' to those of a '251' of today as one would place the *Great Northern* of 1922 in the same power classification as *Golden Eagle* or *Silver Link*.

One of the Ivatt small-boilered Atlantics, No 984, at York south locomotive yard. (*F. Moore*)

In 1911 the Great Northern was a more interesting line to a lover

The 2.20 pm ex-Kings Cross Anglo-Scottish express passing the old, long-dismantled station at Holloway and Caledonian Road, hauled by large Atlantic No 278 (non-superheater). (*Author's collection*)

of historic locomotives than to a train-running enthusiast. If the lightly-loaded crack expresses, such as the 2 pm from Leeds to Kings Cross, and the short-lived 2.15 pm down Yorkshire flyer, be omitted, the majority of the main line services, and the Scotch expresses in particular, had a most leisurely collection of timings. The Ivatt Atlantics, then without superheaters, were indifferent in their performance, and although never piloted, often fell to but little over 30 mph with 300-350 ton loads up the long 1 in 200 banks, with the result that lost time was common. More entertaining running occurred on trains hauled by 4-4-0s and the various single-driver types; 4-4-0s were often used on the Scotch expresses north of Grantham, and in 1910-11 the 5.30 pm down Newcastle diner, usually only six coaches beyond Grantham, was almost invariably hauled by a single over this section. The four-coach 2.15 pm down, which covered the 156 miles from Kings Cross to Doncaster in 165 min, was usually worked by a Stirling 2-2-2, through the famous 2 pm up from Leeds, normally five or six cars, was hauled by an Atlantic; this train had both the

One of the Ivatt superheater 4-4-0s, which were on regular East Coast express working in 1911. Engine No 58 is here seen working a down stopping train north of Hadley Woods. (*Author's collection*)

This photograph of Ivatt 4-4-0 No 1338 shows the turntable at the old passenger sidings at Kings Cross. It was not large enough to turn the Pacifics when they were built, and at first they had to go out to Hornsey for turning. (W.J. Reynolds)

longest and one of the fastest runs on the GNR—Wakefield to Kings Cross, 179.8 miles, in 187 min. The fastest train was the up Manchester express leaving Grantham at 7.48 pm, which was allowed 110 min for the 105.5 miles to Kings Cross; but the load rarely exceeded four coaches.

Owing to the agreement between the East and West Coast companies the day Scotch expresses were timed very slowly over the Great Northern; the 10 o'clock of Flying Scotsman took 120 min from Kings Cross to Grantham, and 98 min for the 82.7 miles thence to York. The 2.20 pm, pre-war counterpart of the 1.20 pm of 1932-9 days, took 122 and 97 minutes respectively over the two stretches. The ordinary Leeds trains did some considerably smarter running, including a Kings Cross-Peterborough run in 82 minutes—55.9 mph average—but their loads were usually not more than 250-300 tons. The Leeds and Manchester flyers were in a class apart, much as the streamlined trains of later years; ordinarily they kept good time.

But in October 1911, the date of Gresley's appointment as Locomotive Superintendent of the GNR, it was not in express passenger motive power that the greatest need lay. A marked trend towards faster goods services all over the country was evident; the GNR was in the forefront of this movement, but strangely enough the company did not possess any engine really suitable for the traffic. In consequence every available passenger tender engine was pressed into service, and Atlantics, 4-4-0s, Stirling 2-4-0s, and even singles could be observed working freight trains. It was this boom in fast goods traffic that began to break down the old principle of 'one driver, one engine', for the fullest use had to be made of locomotives such as the large Atlantics, most of

which included a fair proportion of fast goods mileage in their regular rosters. But the use of other types could be regarded only as a temporary measure pending the construction of suitable engines. Such was the Great Northern's need that for the first ten years of Mr Gresley's chieftainship at Doncaster all new engines turned out were intended for freight service.

The first new type to appear was actually an Ivatt design, a 0-6-0 superheater goods, with 5 ft 2 in wheels, and having the same fine-steaming boiler as the '51' class 4-4-0 express engine. They had cylinders 19 in × 26 in, and although the boiler was dimensionally the same, having 1,230 sq ft of heating surface, the work-

Large Atlantic No 281, non-superheated, passes Holloway on the 2.20 pm Scotsman in 1911. (*F.E. Mackay*)

An Ivatt fast goods engine of 1908: a 5 ft 8 in 0-6-0 of the No 1 class, No 3004, formerly No 4, in LNER livery. (*W.H. Whitworth*)

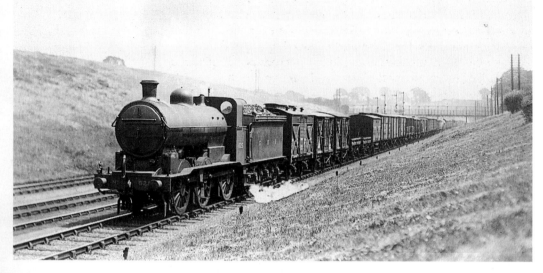

The first GNR class to appear in the Gresley regime was actually an Ivatt design of 5 ft 2 in goods, here seen working a very heavy down train at Oakleigh Park; engine No 625. (*H. Gordon Tidey*)

Gresley's first new design, the 5 ft 8 in superheater express goods engine of 1912. (*British Railways*)

ing pressure was 170 lb per sq in against 160 lb in the 4-4-0s. The first batch, of 15, came out in 1911 and were numbered 521-535; by successive additions, which continued up to 1921, the class now musters 110 strong. Their present numbers are 3521-3610, and 3621-3640, and they are now LNER class 'J6.' The later examples have Robinson superheaters.

The '536' class, as the foregoing engines were usually called, were followed early in 1912 by another goods locomotive design. This, now class 'J2', was also a superheater 0-6-0, but having wheels no less than 5 ft 8 in diameter. In this respect they were similar to Ivatt's No 1 class, built in 1908, but the boiler, cylinders and motion were the same as that of the '536' class. Ten were turned out, Nos 71-80, and were immediately successful. They worked the York-London through goods nightly, and also had a

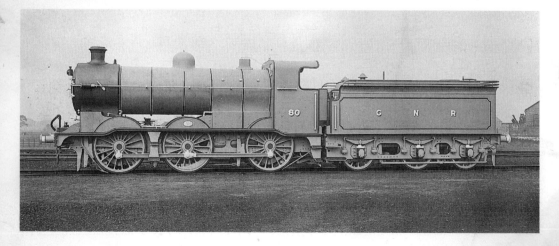

long turn from Peterborough to Manchester. Like the 'No 1' class they were real mixed traffic engines, and at times of pressure took turns on passenger working, excursions and such like, which in those days were not timed at particularly high speeds.

But an 0-6-0 locomotive is not ideal for duties needing speeds of 60 mph or more, no matter how well aligned the road may be. In preparing a new design to meet contemporary needs, therefore, Gresley followed the general trend of British practice at the time for mixed traffic work, and chose the Mogul wheel arrangement. Since the advent in 1899-1901 of the imported 2-6-0s on the Midland, Great Central, and Great Northern, the Mogul was in many quarters looked upon as an undesirable Yankee intrusion. By the year 1912, however, its popularity had been firmly assured by Churchward's '43XX' class on the Great Western, and the new Great Northern engines appeared almost contemporaneously with 2-6-0s on the Brighton, Caledonian, and Glasgow & South Western; not many years later yet another example appeared on the SE&CR. Gresley's engine was described by *The Railway Magazine* of the day as 'a No 1 class 0-6-0 with the addition of a pony truck'; but actually the new type was a far greater departure, and as the parents of a large and successful family of engines the Moguls of 1912 are worthy of special attention.

Ten of the type were built, and numbered 1630 to 1639. Their leading dimensions were: cylinders, 20 in × 26 in, coupled wheels 5 ft 8 in diameter, total heating surface 1,420 sq ft, grate area 24.5 sq ft, working pressure 170 lb per sq in. The principal feature was the front end; Walschaerts valve gear was used, working 10 in diameter piston-valves. The valve setting was carefully arranged so as to give a large exhaust opening when the engine was running well linked-up. Apart from the outside Walschaerts gear and the high raised running plate their appearance was thoroughly Great Northern, and the footplate arrangements unaltered from

The first of the Great Northern Moguls, No 1630, later LNER Class 'K1'. (*British Railways*)

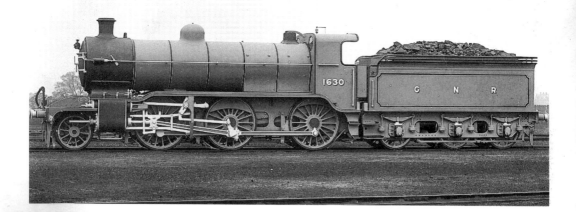

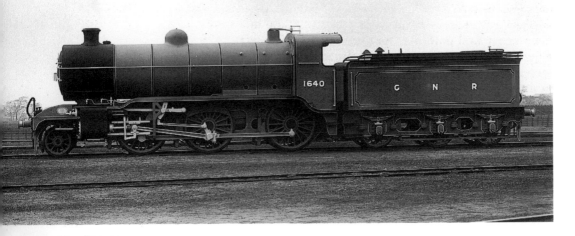

First of the larger-boilered two-cylinder Moguls, No 1640, introduced in 1914, later LNER Class 'K2'. (*British Railways*)

standard practice since Stirling days, the characteristic feature of which was the pull-out type of regulator working in a horizontal plane.

The Moguls of 1912 were not unduly long in showing what they could do; they worked the fast night goods to Doncaster, a 'lodging' turn, and a great variety of mixed traffic jobs, including express passenger trains at times of pressure. In the early days of the war they were often requisitioned for ambulance train workings. If there was a weakness in their design it lay in the boiler, which in proportion to the cylinder dimensions was by Great Northern standards on the small side; the next batch, which came out in 1914, had boilers of 5 ft 6 in diameter, instead of 4 ft 8 in, though the cylinders remained the same. No 1640 was the pioneer of a series numbering 75 engines; their present designation is class 'K2', but on the GNR they formed class 'E1'. As wartime trainloads increased and schedules were eased out, they were sometimes to be seen on regular express turns, but usually there was far too much in the way of fast goods, munition, and troop trains for them to be spared as deputies for the Atlantics. Indeed, they have never seemed quite at home on express working, but as fast freight engines they were second to none at the time of construction.

Since the grouping took place all the '1630s' have been rebuilt as 'K2s', and the sphere of activity of the latter class has been greatly extended, to East Anglia and over the arduous gradients of the West Highland line.

Great locomotive power was needed for other classes of freight service too. The coal traffic between Peterborough and London had already grown to large dimensions, so much so that the Ivatt '401' class 0-8-0s, though satisfactory engines in themselves, were being worked at near their full capacity. Gresley's new design of

1913, the '456' class of 2-8-0s, was a logical development both of the previous 0-8-0s and the '1630' class Moguls, designed for the heaviest freight service. The pony truck, in addition to supporting a heavy and powerful front end, provided a degree of flexibilty in the vehicle that is especially valuable for freight working on a route like the GNR main line, with its frequent diversions from fast to slow road and vice versa.

As motive power units the '456' class (LNER Class 'O1') proved as good as their ample dimensions suggest. Their cylinders were 21 in × 28 in, and in combination with 4 ft 8 in coupled wheels, and a working pressure of 170 lb per sq in, they gave the class a nominal tractive effort of 31,000 lb at 85 per cent of the working pressure. The boiler was the largest Doncaster had produced up to that time, the barrel being 15 ft 5 in long, and 5 ft 6 in diameter,

Cab view of a 'K2' Mogul showing the pull-out regulator, lever reverser, and the generally spartan appearance. (*British Railways*)

One of the first Gresley 2-8-0 heavy freight engines, two-cylinder type, introduced in 1913. (*British Railways*)

and the heating surface of the tubes alone was 1,922 sq ft. Unlike the first Moguls, these 2-8-0s were fitted with Robinson superheaters; a high degree of superheat was evidently aimed at, for the heating surface provided, 570 sq ft, was unusually large for that period. The grate area of these engines was 27 sq ft; adhesion weight 67½ tons; and total weight of engine and tender in working order 119¼ tons. Equipment included 10-in diameter piston valves, as in the Moguls, and the Weir feedwater heater and feed pump. In outward appearance the engines remained faithful to Great Northern traditions, and the Stirling type of regulator handle still featured among the footplate fittings. Thus in the short space of three years Gresley had produced four eminently good designs, three of which, the '71' class 0-6-0s, the '1640' class Moguls and the 2-8-0s were suitable for extensive building if the need arose. Actually they were used merely to meet the immediate requirements of the moment, while still more successful designs were being worked out.

2

GNR, 1915-21

By the beginning of 1915 immediate needs had been met, and Great Northern locomotive history was just entering an interesting transition stage. All over the country new locomotive types were being produced; on all hands superheating was being hailed as the final and conclusive answer to the exponents of compounding, yet on the GNR nothing very much seemed to be happening, outwardly at any rate, in the realm of express passenger motive power. Elsewhere one of the most strongly marked trends of the time was the introduction of multi-cylindered single-expansion locomotives. By 1914 the Great Western had practically standardised the four-cylinder system for crack express engines; the LNWR 'Claughtons' were out and doing good work, by the standards then prevailing, while the Great Northern's own historic partner, the North Eastern, had already turned out a considerable variety of three-cylinder simple designs.

Throughout the Gresley régime close study of contemporary practice, both at home and overseas, has been applied to design at Doncaster works, and in the early years of his chieftainship it is not surprising, in view of what was taking place elsewhere in the country, that Gresley made some experiments with multi-cylindered locomotives. The first step was the complete rebuilding, in 1915, of Atlantic No 279, as a four-cylinder simple; this engine was one of the standard Ivatt '251' class, having two cylinders 18¾ in diameter by 24 in stroke. As rebuilt the engine was provided with four cylinders 15 in diameter by 26 in stroke—a 40 per cent increase in cylinder volume—and the boiler was modified by the fitting of a 24-element Robinson superheater (instead of the previous 18-element one) affording 427 sq ft of heating surface. This heating surface was the same as that of the original Ivatt superheater Atlantics of the 1452-1461 series. No 279 was fitted with the Walschaerts valve gear, but only two sets were provided, the valves of the inside cylinders being actuated by rocking shafts driven off the tail rods of the outside cylinder valve spindles. This rebuilding increased the weight of No 279 from the original 65½ tons to 73½ tons. As rebuilt No 279 was in nominal tractive effort the most powerful express engine on the GNR, though curiously enough she never came into the lime-light to the same extent as the ordinary '251' class. In her second rebuild, in 1938, as a two-cylinder engine with Walschaerts valve gear, she still remains unique among the Atlantics. As now running, No 3279 (GNR No. 279) has two cylinders 20 in × 26 in, but she is not the first GNR Atlantic to be so equipped. In 1917 the four-cylinder compound No 1300, built by the Vulcan Foundry Co Ltd, was converted into a two-cylinder simple by Gresley, and a pair of standard 20 in × 26 in cylinders, as used on the 'K1' and 'K2' 2-6-0s, was fitted. The original boiler, after twelve years of continuous service in express traffic, was retained and modified for superheated steam; a 22-element superheater was fitted, having a heating surface of 280 sq ft. The working pressure was reduced from the 200 lb per sq in of the original compound to 170 lb per sq in. No 1300, as converted, was nominally more powerful than the standard superheated Atlantics of the '251' class, and for a time during the early months of 1918 she was working on the 5.30 pm Newcastle express from Kings Cross. With a nightly load of over 400 tons, and an allowance of 125 min to cover the 105.5 miles from Kings Cross to Grantham, it was a difficult turn. Another Gresley conversion was that of the Ivatt four-cylinder compound Atlantic No 1421, into a standard superheater '251' in 1920.

It was not until May 1918, three years after Gresley's interesting experimental rebuilding on No 279, that the next multi-cylindered engine appeared on the GNR; this was the first three-cylinder 2-8-0, No 461. The suitability of three-cylinder propulsion for heavy freight working had already been demonstrated on the North Eastern Railway, where Wilson Worsdell's Class 'X' 4-8-0 tanks were operating successfully in the Erimus hump yard. The system equally has advantages in such duties as the haulage of the Peterborough-London coal trains, in which a locomotive may have to start heavy loads from rest against a 1 in 200 gradient. A more even crank effort is obtained with a three-cylinder engine, having its cranks set at 120 degrees to each other, than with the two-cylinder arrangement, in which the cranks are at right-angles to each other, and a smoother start is possible; it is not so much a matter of power as the way in which that power is applied to the drawbar.

No 461 carried a boiler identical with that of the '456' class, but the two 21 in × 28 in cylinders were replaced by three cylinders, 18 in × 26 in, arranged in line and driving the second pair of coupled wheels. The connecting rods are thus much shorter than in the earlier engines, and the cylinders are steeply inclined. But at the time of construction the outstanding feature of No 461 was the valve gear. All previous three-cylinder simple locomotives built in this country—Robinson's Great Central 0-8-4 humping tanks, his one three-cylinder simple Atlantic, No 1090, and the various North Eastern types—used three sets of valve gear. By the mechanism illustrated in principle in Fig 1, however, Gresley eliminated one set of valve motion. As applied to No 461 the details were rather different, and are shown in Fig 2. The cross-sectional view of the cylinders and valves shows why it was necessary to place the valve casing for the inside cylinder in a different transverse plane from that of the two outside cylinders; this disposition involved the use of vertical levers in the derived valve motion, and made the layout of the gear rather more complicated. Later, however, the arrangement shown in Fig 1 became the standard form of the gear. Another novel feature of this engine has since become standard on all the largest LNER locomotives; this is the vertical-screw reversing gear. The adjustment of cut-off is facilitated by the inclusion of ball bearings in the screw mounting.

No 461 was put to work on the Peterborough-London coal trains and very soon showed a certain superiority over the '456' class, particularly in starting. In the haulage of a heavy coal train, weighing 1,300 tons gross behind the tender, a cut-off of 45 per cent, with the regulator something below one-half open, was needed to maintain an average of 22½ mph over the 15 miles from Huntingdon to Sandy, on a typical journey. In getting away, and on the 1 in 200 banks, as much as 60 per cent cut-off was customary. But in spite of the successful working of No 461, building of the '456' class two-cylinder 2-8-0s continued.

The next three-cylinder engine was another advance upon former practice, and its advent was surrounded by just enough secrecy to set going a flood of rumours. Soon after the armistice

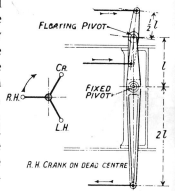

Figure 1 Standard Gresley derived valve motion.

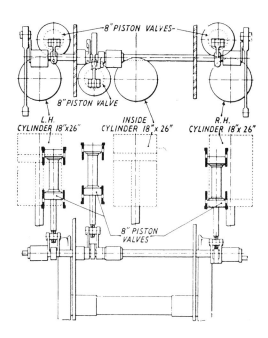

Figure 2 Layout of the valve gear on engine No 461.

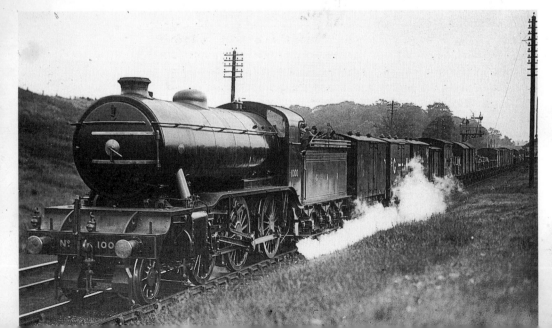

of November 1918, the news got about that a 'super' main line locomotive was under construction at Doncaster; everything pointed to a Prairie at least, if not a Pacific, and then, early in 1920, No· 1000 came out, the first of the three-cylinder Moguls. This remarkable engine created quite a stir at the time by reason of her boiler; up till then a diameter of 5 ft 6 in had been regarded as the maximum conveniently possible within the British loading gauge, whereas the boiler of the Gresley three-cylinder Mogul was 6 ft diameter over the smallest ring, and accommodated 217 tubes of 1¾ in outside diameter. The other leading boiler dimensions are: heating surface, tubes, 1,719 sq ft; firebox, 182 sq ft; 32-element superheater , 407 sq ft. The grate area is 28 sq ft and the working pressure is 180 lb per sq in—the latter a slight advance upon pre-

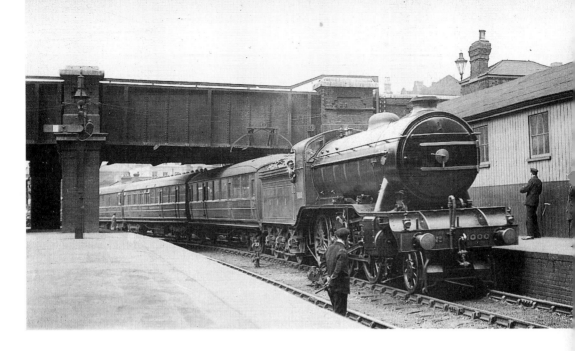

No 1000 entering Kings
Cross with a heavy up
express. (*H. Gordon
Tidey*)

vious Gresley practice.

There were further features of interest in the front end, for not only was the cylinder volume far in excess of that of any eight-wheel engine then at work on any other British railway, but there was also an alteration in the arrangement of the valve gear. The three cylinders were 18½ in diameter × 26 in stroke, and by inclining the central cylinder at a much steeper angle than the outside ones it was possible so to arrange the valves that the simple horizontal rocking lever mechanism (Fig 1), subsequently standardised, could be used for actuating the piston-valve of the inside cylinder. This was found to be a great improvement upon the layout of the gear used on the 2-8-0 engine No 461. Another detail destined to become standard practice on the LNER which made its first appearance on No 1000 was the provision of twin regulator handles, one on each side of the cab; the handle on the fireman's side is often of great value when a locomotive is being manoeuvred in a busy yard. The outward appearance of the cab remained faithful to Great Northern traditions, though nowadays of course only a tiny minority of ten in the great regiment of 'K3' Moguls possess this outward sign of true Doncaster lineage. The original engines, though intended mainly for fast goods working, came into the limelight during the coal strike of 1921, when they tackled express passenger trains loading up to 20 bogie vehicles on the fastest schedules then operating between Kings Cross and Doncaster, and showed themselves capable of 75 mph on stretches like that from Stoke summit down to Peterborough.

In the meantime much important progress was being made in the modernisation of existing types. Quite apart from the super-heating of the '251' class Atlantics, to which special reference is made later, the performance of a number of Ivatt types was

The second three-cylinder Mogul, No 1001, in photographic grey at Doncaster. (*British Railways*)

improved. Larger boilers, with superheaters, were fitted to some of the 4-4-0 express locomotives; a number of the small Atlantics and the 0-8-0 goods engines were also superheated, and one of the most interesting conversions was that applied to the Ivatt 0-8-2 tanks. After their departure from the London suburban district these engines were transferred to Colwick for use in the coal and goods marshalling yards; here they were engaged on purely local traffic. But the superheating of some of this class enabled them to work heavy coal trains between Colwick and the New England yard, Peterborough, a run of 47 miles. The saturated 0-8-2s were unable to undertake this turn as the tanks carried insufficient water to supply their increased consumption over that of the super-heated engines. The fitting of superheaters to low-speed short-haul engines was not, however, inaugurated on these 0-8-2 tanks.

The former No 1001, in LNER livery and numbered 4001, on an up fast goods near Stevenage. (*O.S. Nock*)

In 1913 a new 0-6-0 shunting tank locomotive of Gresley's own design was put into service; the first of this class, No 157, used saturated steam, but a later one, No 167 (put into service in 1914), was superheated. The respective leading dimensions are: cylinders, 18½ in × 26 in; wheels, 4 ft 8 in diameter; working pressure, 175 and 170 lb per sq in; total heating surface, 980 and 932.5 sq ft, the latter including 171 sq ft provided by the superheater; grate area 17.8 sq ft; weight in working order, including 1,500 gallons of water and 3 tons of coal, 56½ tons. These original engines are now LNER Class 'J51'. They were the forerunners of the numerous standard 0-6-0 shunting tanks of the LNER, which are classed 'J50' and are generally similar to the engine of 1913, except that the boiler is larger, 4 ft 5 in diameter against 4 ft 2 in in the original engine, with a total heating surface of 1,119 sq ft;

One of the first of the Gresley 0-6-2 superheater tank engines, No 1763, in GNR passenger colours. (*Author's collection*)

An 0-6-2 tank piloting a large Atlantic with a heavy down express leaving Kings Cross. Engine No 1727 would have been detached at Potters Bar. (*H. Gordon Tidey*)

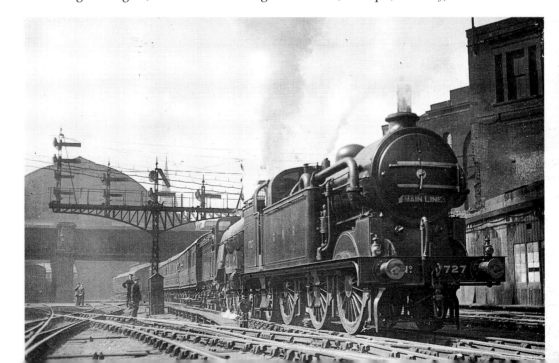

‘N2’ 0-6-2 tank No 4610 on the City Widened Lines with a suburban train from Moorgate Street. (*W.J. Reynolds*)

‘N2’ 0-6-2 tank No 2664, with long condenser pipes as first fitted. (*W.J. Reynolds*)

the grate area, however, is slightly less at 16¼ sq ft. With a larger coal bunker to hold 4¾ tons, the ‘J50’ is slightly heavier, weighing 58 tons. It is not superheated.

In 1913 Gresley designed his twin-tube superheater. There are 34 flue tubes, 4 in external diameter, each element being in two flue tubes. By this arrangement greater evaporation and superheating areas are obtained; the saturated header is located above the level of the flue tubes, and the superheated header below. How successful this layout proved in practice was shown in one of Gresley's last designs for the GNR, one that stands out from the general line of continuity in practice displayed in the locomotives built by him up to that time, and subsequently. The superheated 0-6-2 passenger tanks, the first of which was turned out in January 1921,

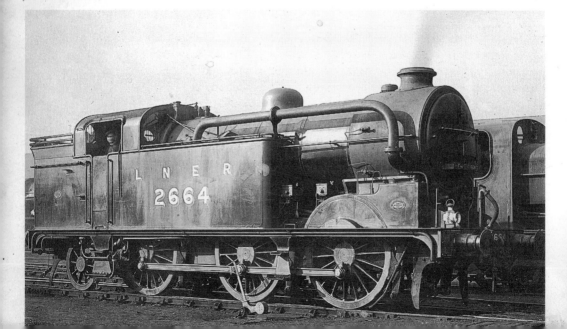

were just a simple straightforward two-cylinder job, well suited to the pressing needs of the London suburban traffic. What appears to be the exceptionally high-line pitch of their boilers is rather an illusion caused by the severe restrictions of the Metropolitan loading gauge which cut the height of the engines working over the widened lines to 12 ft 7 in, and made it necessary to use unusually squat boiler mountings. The leading dimensions of this class are as follows: cylinders 19 in diameter by 26 in stroke; coupled wheels 5 ft 8 in diameter; total heating surface, 1,205 sq ft, of which the 17-element superheater contributes 207 sq ft; grate area, 19 sq ft; working pressure, 170 lb per sq in; weight in working order, 70¼ tons, including 2,000 gallons of water and 4 tons of coal. Such preliminary experience as was necessary had already been obtained by the superheating of one of the numerous Ivatt 0-6-2 tanks (LNER Class 'N1') No 1598, and the new locomotives, which were a logical development of Ivatt's design, were drafted to the most arduous suburban duties the moment they were broken in.

Sixty of these engines, now, LNER class 'N2', were turned out very rapidly, 10 from Doncaster, and 50 by the North British Locomotive Co Ltd, the original numbers being 1606-15 (Doncaster) and 1721-70. Further examples, without condensing apparatus, have been built since grouping for suburban service around Glasgow and Edinburgh. They are not only powerful engines for their size, but also speedy. Before the days of the Pacifics they were sometimes requisitioned to pilot main line expresses out to Potters Bar; while their hill-climbing feats, over the tremendous gradients of the High Barnet branch, though a commonplace today, were exceptional when they first came out. Up the 2½ miles at 1 in 59-63 from Finsbury Park, for example, with the trains that pass a number of stations, speeds usually rise to 30 mph or so with loads of 160 tons.

Mention of the Ivatt 0-6-2 tanks in connection with the experimental work prior to the building of the 'N2s', recalls the equipment by Gresley in 1915 of two of them with armouring for use in coastal armoured trains. They could be driven from the footplate or from either end of the train in which they were placed in the middle. Further special locomotive work, carried out at Doncaster during the war of 1914-18 under Gresley's direction, involved the modification of a number of 0-6-0 tender engines (LNER 'J3' class) so that they could exhaust through the chimney, behind the tender, or condense into the tender. Thus equipped, they were used in forward areas in France.

The first of a new batch of three-cylinder 2-8-0s came out in 1921; they differed from No 461 in having the alteration to the derived valve gear that had proved so satisfactory in the '1000' class Moguls. No 477 was the first of the new series, now LNER Class

Above Three-cylinder 2-8-0 No 3485, Class 'O2', with a long train of coal empties climbing to Potters Bar. (*James R. Clark*)

Above right Three-cylinder 2-8-0 No 3490, Class 'O2', at Hornsey sheds. (*W.J. Reynolds*)

Right The first Great Northern large-boilered Atlantic, as LNER No 3251, on an up express south of Grantham. (*M.W. Earley*)

'O2', in which the principal dimensional changes from No 461 were an increase in boiler pressure from 170 to 180 lb per sq in, and the enlargement of the cylinders from 18 to 18½ in diameter. The cylinder disposition is almost identical with that of the '1000' class, the inside cylinder being steeply inclined so that the three steam chests can be arranged in line. This type is now the standard heavy freight engine of the LNER.

While these new types were being introduced, an important modification to the large Atlantics was being applied one by one to the whole class. The ten superheater engines built by Ivatt, Nos 1452-1461, showed a definite though not very great superiority over the saturated variety, particularly in uphill work, but their work fell considerably short of the feats to which we are now accustomed. They were the victims of a mistaken conception of superheating. Ivatt attempted to exploit the principle purely for the reduction of boiler maintenance, reducing the working pressure from the 175 lb of the saturated engines to 150 lb per sq in, so that although the cylinders were increased in diameter from 18¾ in to 20 in, the power of the engines was barely altered. There were steaming troubles, too—a thing almost unheard of with the '251s' of today, or with the original non-superheater engines. When a start was made with the superheating of the original Ivatt Atlantics bolder measures were taken, the boiler pressure being retained practically at the former figure of 175 lb per sq in. The

process of transformation was gradual, for many of the engines at first retained their slide-valves, while others were fitted with new 8-in diameter piston-valves. The first engines to be equipped were provided with 24-element superheaters, having the same amount of heating surface—427 sq ft—as Nos 1452-61 and the four-cylinder engine No 279. In 1919, however, No 1403 was fitted with a 32-element superheater, having 568 sq ft of heating surface. This variety later became standard for the whole class, and those engines which for a time had 24-element superheaters were subsequently modified. By no means all of them have been fitted with piston-valves, however; the slide-valve engines, which retain their 18¾ in cylinders, are now mostly to be found on the Great Central section.

Credit for the wonderful work of the '251' class is usually bestowed in its entirety upon Ivatt, but the modifications that transformed them from a type of moderate and at times indifferent performance into some of the most capable engines of their size and weight that have ever run on British metals were carried out during the Gresley regime. The piston-valve engines, with 20-in cylinders, have done the finest work, but before the second war the Sheffield drivers used to get excellent running out of their slide-valve engines. It was during the later years of the 1914-1919 war that the full haulage capacity of the superheated '251s' was first demonstrated, and although those early feats, by the 24-element superheater engines, have since been totally eclipsed by the still more capable '251s' of today, on very much faster sched-

Large Atlantic No 1447, as superheated by Gresley and fitted with a 32-element apparatus, on the 5.30 pm Newcastle express at Hadley Wood. (F.E. Mackay)

ules, one can quite well imagine the thrill of a run like that of No 1407, which, with the 1.40 pm down and a load of 575 tons, ran from Potters Bar to Peterborough, start to stop, 63.7 miles, in 74 minutes. Still finer was the 1921 coal strike exploit of No 290 in working a load of 600 tons from Peterborough to Kings Cross, 76.4 miles, in 92 min 35 sec. What is more, they were never piloted, save from King's Cross to Potters Bar; this luxury, however, was permitted only when the load exceeded a modest 66 axles.

One of the 'K2' Moguls, No 1674, fitted for oil burning during the 1921 coal strike. (*British Railways*)

3

The 'A1' Pacifics

The locomotive history of the Great Northern Railway, as an individual concern, closed in spectacular fashion with the completion of the first two Pacific engines, 1470 and 1471. These behemoths fitly concluded a remarkable locomotive lineage turned out of Doncaster works between 1867 and 1922; their superiority over the '251' class, both in mere size and tractive power, was in just about the same ratio as that of the first Ivatt Atlantic, No 990, over the Stirling 8-footers. Yet the trend of development had been so clearly marked in the past that the proportions of the new engines were no surprise. In view of the success of the '251s' it was hardly likely that the Wootten firebox would be abandoned, and nothing less than six-coupled wheels would have been adequate to cope with the increasing East Coast loads. The girth of the boiler could be anticipated from the 6 ft boilers fitted to the '1000' class Moguls; three-cylinder propulsion, with derived motion for the inside cylinder, was almost a certainty, and the only thing that remained in doubt was the wheel arrangement. A 2-6-2 was actually contemplated at one time; the design of pony truck used on the Moguls had already proved suitable for high speed running, but as the design took shape a leading bogie was decided upon, and No 1470 *Great Northern* was the result.

Many problems beset the designer who puts on the road a machine that embodies such bold advances upon previous practice, if he is to produce a thoroughly sound job from the railway point of view; the country had already witnessed the spectacle of a great engine so limited in her sphere of activity as to be more of a liability than an asset to her owners. The length of the new Pacific was one of the problems in design, for although the Great Northern main line boasts one of the finest alignments in the country, matters are not so favourable to a long engine in the immediate neighbourhood of Kings Cross. By the use of heat-treated nickel-chrome steel having a tensile strength some 50 per cent greater than ordinary mild steel it was possible to make the connecting and coupling rods much lighter than usual, and thus the effect of the unbalanced forces due to the reciprocating mechanism were reduced. The fine riding qualities of the class, which have to be sampled on the footplate to be fully appreciated, are

due to the present springing arrangement, which was arrived at only after trials of several different layouts; uncompensated plate springs are used for all three pairs of coupled wheels.

The leading dimensions of No 1470 are well known, but are included for reference purposes: three cylinders 20 in diameter by 26 in stroke; coupled wheels 6 ft 8 in diameter; total heating surface 3,455 sq ft; grate area 41¼ sq ft; working pressure 180 lb per sq in; total weight of engine and tender in working order, with 8 tons of coal and 5,000 gallons of water, 148¾ tons. The unusually large grate area of 41¼ sq ft caused some shaking of heads by people who thought the fireman's burden was becoming over-whelming, but in actual fact the Gresley Pacifics are not difficult to fire; the accurate wristwork needed to shoot the coal into the back corners of the grate calls for knack rather than brute force.

The new engines were not long in showing what they could do. On Sunday 3 September 1922, a special test run was made

The first Gresley Pacific, No 1470 *Great Northern*, in a photograph autographed by the designer. (*British Railways*))

The second Pacific, No 1471, then unnamed, on a 610-ton test run near New Southgate in 1922. (*H. Gordon Tidey*)

Engine No 1471, after being named *Sir Frederick Banbury,* on the 1.30 pm Leeds and Bradford express near Hadley Wood. (*O.S. Nock*)

with No 1471, then unnamed, on which a train of 20 vehicles weighing 610 tons behind the tender was worked over the 105.5 miles from Kings Cross to Grantham in 122 min. The highlights of this performance were a time of 23 min from Hitchin to Huntingdon, an average speed of 70 mph, and a fine climb to Stoke with an average speed of 45 mph up the final 3 miles from Corby.

In ordinary service the Pacifics were not called upon to perform anything like such strenuous work as this. During the late autumn and winter of 1922 they were usually on the 4 pm and 5.40 pm trains from Kings Cross. The former, in deference to its traditionally heavy load, was then allowed no less than 101 min to Peterborough, but the 5.40 pm, with an average load of 500 tons and 87 min allowed for the Kings Cross-Peterborough run, was a stiff proposition for those days. The results obtained from Nos 1470 and 1471 were sufficiently good for a further ten Pacifics to be ordered before the Great Northern became merged in the LNER group, but the first of the new series—the famous No 4472—was not turned out of Doncaster works until January 1923. But by this time the supremacy of the 1470s was being challenged, and from within the same group, too; the first of Sir Vincent Raven's still larger Pacifics had just been turned out at Darlington works, and although differing radically from the Great Northern design, had about the same tractive effort.

My first personal experience of the Gresley Pacifics was in June 1923, when I travelled from Kings Cross to Doncaster behind No 1473. For quite a trivial reason I decided, to my lasting regret, to go by the 4 pm instead of the 5.40; that very day the 5.40 was worked by No 2400, a North Eastern Pacific, afterwards named

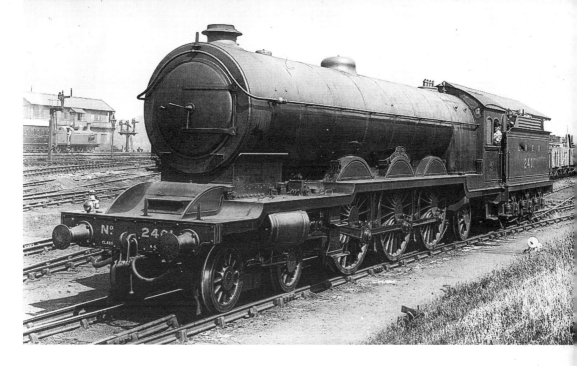

City of Newcastle, in one of a series of trials in competition with Great Northern type Pacifics. Even allowing for her driver being strange to the road, No 2400 did not do too well; there was a lot of trouble with heating, and on the trips when all went well the engine had difficulty in handling the turns that the Gresley Pacifics were working with complete success. For example, on the 10.51 am from Doncaster to Kings Cross, with a load of 453 tons from the start, and another coach added at Grantham, the average speed inclusive of stops was 54 mph. To do this the coal consumption was just over 50 lb per mile, the average cut-off throughout was 40 per cent, and with the boiler pressure maintained at an average of 165 lb per sq in the steam chest pressure averaged 129 lb per sq in; the latter is equal to a regulator roughly five-eighths open. It was on the strength of results such as this, and the superiority over the North Eastern 4-6-2s, that a further batch of 40 Gres-

One of the Raven Pacifics of the former North Eastern Railway which ran competitive trials against Gresley Pacifics in 1923: engine No 2401 at York. (*Real Photos Co Ltd*)

Pacific No 1478, then unnamed, on the new turntable at Kings Cross. (*W.J. Reynolds*)

ley Pacifics was put in hand by the LNER for general service throughout the East Coast route.

Then, in the autumn of 1923, the first of the Great Western Railway 4-6-0 'Castle' locomotives appeared. The tractive effort of this new class, 31,625 lb, gave them a lead of nearly 2,000 lb over both the LNER varieties of 4-6-2, and substantiated a claim that the GWR 'Castles' were the most powerful express locomotives in the country. But the LNER refused to accept such a claim without question, and Doncaster was undoubtedly the prime mover in suggesting a scientific trial, with subsequent interchange of results. Unfortunately, from the engineering standpoint, the 'challenge' was taken up with such gusto that technical achievement became rather lost in a welter of partisanship. Railway enthusiasts, and indeed the general public, had in some measure been prepared for this event. At the British Empire Exhibition at Wembley in 1924, No 4472, named *Flying Scotsman* specially for exhibition, and No 4073, *Carphilly Castle*, stood on adjacent stands. It seemed as if the two types were fated to try conclusions sooner or later.

The chance actually came, after a week of trial running, from 27 April to 2 May 1925, and between Paddington and Plymouth the GWR staged some spectacular performances. Engine No 4074, *Caldicot Castle*, in charge of a driver who was to the GWR of that time what Bill Sparshatt became to the LNER in more recent times, twice within the week brought in The Limited a quarter of an hour before time. Feats such as these were bound to confuse the issue, and placed the competing LNER engine No 4474, whose driver had been instructed to run to schedule, at a disadvantage. The West of England main line between Reading and Plymouth is an exceptionally awkward road for a stranger, and to be practically

Engine No 4472 *Flying Scotsman* specially painted with a crest on the cab side ready for display at the British Empire Exhibition in 1924. (*British Railways*)

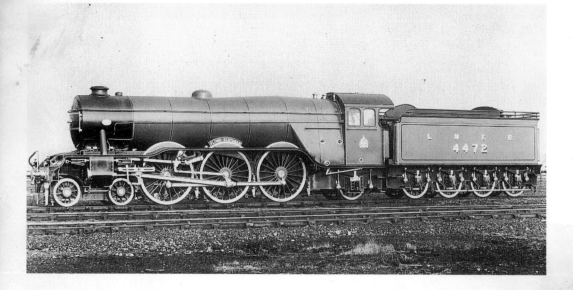

on time at Plymouth on their very first trip with the down Limited
was a masterly piece of locomotive handling by the LNER crew.
What is more, the coal consumption was only 50 lb per mile,
which, even allowing for the higher calorific value of Welsh coal,
was very little above the normal Pacific figure. In the hectic excite-
ment of what was generally regarded as a purely sporting con-
test, however, such considerations counted for little with the
general public and the popular press.

But there is no disguising the fact that the LNER was beaten
on its own road. The locomotive principally concerned was No
2545, which has since been named *Diamond Jubilee*, and was a hurriedly picked second string after the first choice, No 4475, had
failed with a hot box. To the chagrin of her supporters No 2545
struck a particularly bad patch and failed to rise even to normal
Pacific standards. The reason is to be found in one of the hundred-
and-one minor ailments that can, on any railway, jaundice locomotive performance; but that such trouble should have developed
in the company's chosen representative during so critical a week
was a piece of extremely bad luck. The Great Western engine—
No 4079 *Pendennis Castle*—certainly took the wind out of the LNER
sails. On trip after trip she lifted her 475-ton trains through Finsbury Park in less than 6 min, and on the fastest run was through
Hatfield in 23 min 25 sec. After that, short cut-offs and light steaming sufficed for speeds of average East Coast quality, and brought
her trains into Peterborough and Doncaster well before time on
each journey. Full details of the times and speeds made on the

Gresley Pacific No 4474, then unnamed, arriving at Paddington with the Cornish Riviera Express. (*Real Photos Co Ltd*)

test runs were published in *The Railway Magazine* for July and August 1925.

The immediate results of the exhange, details of the running and certain technical items were published by the companies concerned soon after the event. Controversy raged around the merits and demerits of the two types for many months afterwards, but much of this centred upon the differences in boiler and firebox. Each is an outstanding design peculiarly suitable for its own class of fuel and service. It is true that the Great Western engine did very well on Yorkshire coal, but a close examination of the logs of her running shows that most of the sparkle and brilliance of her work took place at the beginning of the journeys; there was never quite the same dash about the Grantham-Doncaster stage as was so noticeable between Kings Cross and Peterborough, and one wonders what might have happened had *Pendennis Castle* essayed the present-day Pacific duty of working through from London to Newcastle or Edinburgh.

The essential difference between the two types lay in the front end—long-travel versus short-travel valves. In a general way it is known that long-travel valves make for economical running and higher speeds, but few if any definite figures have been published to show exactly where the difference lies. With short-travel valves both the admission and exhaust ports are never more than partly open when a locomotive is running well linked up, and the earlier the point of cut-off is brought the smaller these openings become. Narrow valve openings severely throttle the steam both at admission and exhaust, and hamper an engine severely; an investigation into the cylinder and valve performance of one of the Midland compounds—generally accepted as a most efficient class—showed

that when running at 68 mph 35 per cent of the total energy of
the steam put through the cylinders was spent in getting through
the admission and exhaust ports. By increasing the length of valve
travel the movement of the valves can be so arranged that the full
width of the exhaust ports is available even when the engine is
linked up to mid gear. For many years British locomotive engineers
were inclined to look askance at the long valve travels of the GWR
on account of the extra wear on valves and liners consequent upon
higher valve speeds. But in many ways the term 'long-travel' valves
is a misnomer; they should, strictly speaking, be called long lap
valves, for when an engine is linked right up and running at 70
mph the actual travel of the valves may well be *less* than that of
a locomotive fitted with short-lap valves and needing to be worked
at comparatively long cut-offs.

After the exchange tests of 1925, the first trial of long-travel valves
was made on the LNER. In 1926 the valve gear of No 4477 *Gay
Crusader* was modified so as to give longer laps and a freer exhaust.
As many as possible of the existing parts of the gear were used
in carrying out this experimental re-arrangement, which
thoroughly justified itself. No 4477 proved decidely more economical than the standard Pacifics. This success prompted a redesign
of the gear, in which the lap was increased from the original 1¼
in to 1⅝ in, and the valve travel in full gear from 4⁹/₁₆ in to 5¾
in; this was tried out early in 1927 on No 2555 *Centenary*. Trials
between this engine and No 2559, with short-travel valves, showed
that the altered gear reduced the coal consumption from roughly

One of the general
service Pacifics, with
cut-down boiler
mountings but having
the original valve gear,
No 2559 *The Tetrarch* on
an up Anglo-Scottish
express near Three
Counties in July 1926.
(*Rail Archive Stephenson,
F.R. Hebron*)

A standard Class 'A1'
Pacific No 2546 *Donovan*
after the improved
valve gear was fitted.
(*Author's collection*)

50 to 38-39 lb per train mile; and from that time onward the whole stud, one by one, had their valve gear altered to the *Centenary* arrangement. The two tables below show the differences between the original and present valve settings.

Tables of valve setting (forward gear)

For Gresley 'A1' Pacifics with three 20 in × 26 in cylinders and 8 in piston valves.

Original setting. Lead $^1/_{16}$ in, steam lap 1½ in, exhaust lap — ¼ in (negative).

Cylinder	Nominal cut off (per cent)	Valve opening (in)		Cut off (per cent)		Exhaust opens (per cent)		Exhaust port opening above full port (in)		Exhaust closes (per cent)	
		F	B	F	B	F	B	F	B	F	B
Outside	25	19/64	19/64	25.9	24	63.4	60.8	1/16	1/16	75.5	77
Centre	25	5/16	5/16	25.9	24.3	64.9	59.9	1/16	1/16	75.7	79.4
Outside	65	31/32	1	67	62.9	85.7	83.3	25/32	23/32	90.8	92.3
Centre	65	29/32	1	64.2	62.2	87	85	3/4	21/32	92.3	92.7

Present setting. Lead ⅛ in, steam lap 1⅜ in, exhaust lap = line and line

Outside	15	12/64	13/64	14.4	15.6	65.6	65.1	5/64	4/64	65.1	65.6
Inside	15	12/64	14/64	15.3	16.5	65.9	65.3	6/64	4/64	65.3	65.9
Outside	25	19/64	20/64	24.3	25.9	72.8	71.6	12/64	11/64	71.6	72.8
Inside	25	18/64	23/64	24.7	25.7	73	71.1	15/64	10/64	71.1	73
Outside	65	13/16	1 1/4	67.3	63.9	89.9	88.2	1 1/8	11/16	88.2	89.9
Inside	65	1 1/8	15/16	64.9	63.7	90.6	89.9	13/16	1	89.9	90.6

The more economical working of the engines was an important factor that contributed much to the feasibility of the London-Edinburgh non-stop running of the Flying Scotsman, which was inaugurated on 1 May 1928. Engine No 4472 *Flying Scotsman* was

transferred from Doncaster shed, where she had been stationed ever since her construction, to Kings Cross specially for this working, and with No 4476 *Royal Lancer* bore the brunt of the non-stop running throughout the summer. The timing of 8¼ hours involved very easy locomotive work, and for that reason was subjected to some disparagement, but the standard of punctuality set was high and the experience gained in this, the greatest feat of locomotive endurance attempted up to that time in this country, paved the way for the more remarkable developments of recent years. As to the performances of the 'A1s', my own log-books reveal run after run of great merit. There is one of Sparshatt's characteristic feats, for example, with engine No 4472 on the up Flying Scotsman; with a load of 565 tons gross behind the tender he ran from Darlington to a signal stop at Poppleton Junction, 42.5 miles, in 40 min 18 sec start to stop, speed averaging exactly 72 mph for the 27 miles from Northallerton to milepost 3. That was in 1933, and on the last lap of another run on the same train a few weeks later, with another noted Kings Cross driver, the late Harry Gutteridge, engine No 4474 *Victor Wild* worked a load of 520 tons through Finsbury Park in 102 min 52 sec from Grantham, 103.0 miles; but for a signal stop at Belle Isle the terminus would have been reached in about 107½ min. Schedule was 114 min.

Then, on a most unlikely occasion, at the close of 1935—a miserable winter's evening of thin drizzling rain—the late W. Payne, yet another well-known Kings Cross driver, made some glorious running with No 2552 *Sansovino*. On the up Scotsman, loading

The up non-stop Flying Scotsman approaching Grantham in 1930 hauled by engine No 4475 *Flying Fox*. (*Rail Archive Stephenson, T.G. Hepburn*)

to 520 tons behind the tender, we were inside 'even time' from the Grantham start as early as Werrington Junction; did the 27 miles from Huntingdon to Hitchin in 24 min 31 sec; and were through Hatfield, 87.8 miles, in 86¾ min, against 91 min then scheduled. Adverse signals delayed us badly at Potters Bar, otherwise we should have reached Kings Cross in 104 min for the 105.5 miles from Grantham. Booked time, 111 min.

Below The down Junior Scotsman, the 10.05 am ex-Kings Cross, in Newcastle with engine No 2569 *Gladiateur*. (*W.G. Greenfield*)

On the footplate I witnessed and interesting example of the ease with which the 'A1s' handled 500-ton loads on the East Coast timings of 1935. No 4476 *Royal Lancer* was the engine, in charge of the crew that made such astonishing records on *Silver Link's* première in September 1935—Driver Taylor and Fireman Luty, of Kings Cross shed. A delay at Offord had made the 1.20 pm Scotsman 10 min late into Grantham, and it is from this point northwards that the run is tabulated overleaf. The timing of 92 min for the 82.7 miles from Grantham to York was not unduly difficult, and there were then drivers in the link who would have attempted to wipe off all the lateness on this one section. On the other hand, such energy was sometimes offset later in the journey by a need to nurse the engine on the usually stiff passage from York to Darlington—especially as in this case, when the wind was on the quarter. Taylor was content with the recovery of 6 min, for 6 min he certainly had 'in the bag' on passing Chaloners Whin Junction, though adverse signals robbed him of just over a minute in approaching York. As a result of this gentler treatment *Royal Lancer* was in first-class form over the North Eastern line, and Northallerton was passed only 3 min behind time. As regards the actual working of the engine, it will be seen that Taylor never used less than 25 per cent cut-off, though it was only in making the very fine start out of York that full regulator was used for any length of time.

Opposite An up Anglo-Scottish express passing Plessey hauled by engine No 4472 *Flying Scotsman*. (*Norman Wilkinson*)

The up Sunday Flying Scotsman leaving the Royal Border Bridge hauled by engine No 2571 *Sunstar*. (*O.S. Nock*)

LNER 3.16 pm Grantham-Darlington

Engine: Class 'A1' 4-6-2 No 4476 *Royal Lancer*
Load: 483 tons tare, 515 tons full
Driver Taylor; Fireman Luty (Kings Cross Shed)

Dist (miles)		Schedule (min)	Actual (min sec)	Speeds (mph)	Regu-later	Cut-off (per cent)	Pressure (lb per sq in) Boiler	Steam chest
0.0	GRANTHAM	0	0 00	—	Full	65	—	—
4.2	Barkston		6 29	60	⅜	25	170	135
9.9	Claypole		11 27	75	⅜	25		
14.6	NEWARK	15	15 23	72	¾	25	175	140
21.9	Crow Park		21 49	66	⅞	25	170	150
28.2	Markham Box		28 40	50	½	25	170	120
			—	68	Shut	25	170	—
33.1	RETFORD	35	33 32	60	⅝	25	170	110
38.4	Ranskill		38 30	67	½	25	170	110
44.0	Mile Post 149½		44 00	51	½	25	170	110
47.7	Black Carr Jc		47 43	65	½	25	170	130
50.5	DONCASTER	53	50 28	60	⅜	25	170	130
54.7	Shaftholme Jc	58	54 38	61½	⅜	25	175	138
60.5	Balne		60 07	64½	⅜	25	175	138
67.5	Brayton Jc		66 55	65	Shut	25	175	138
68.9	SELBY	74	68 40	25‡	⅞	30	160	150
73.0	Riccall		74 30	53	⅞	25	160	150
80.7	Chaloners Whin Jc		82 43	60	⅞	25	160	150
			Sigs					
82.7	YORK	92	87 25*	—	—	—	—	—
0.0		0	0 00	—	Full	65	—	—
1.6	Poppleton Jc		3 46	—	Full	25	175	165
5.5	Beningbrough		8 30	57	Full	25	175	165
11.2	Alne		13 58	66½	Full	25	170	160
18.0	Sessay		20 22	62	⅞	25	175	140
22.2	THIRSK	25	24 23	67	⅞	25	175	140
30.0	NORTHALLERTON	33	31 45	61	⅞	25	177	140
			pws	25	Full	35	177	140
38.9	Greyholme Jc		43 32	54½	½	25	160	115
41.5	Croft Spa		46 13	64½	½	25	160	115
			Sigs					
44.1	DARLINGTON	48	50 40¶	—	—	—	—	—

‡ Severe service slack   * Net time 86¼ min   ¶ Net time 46 min

Since 1937 the work of the streamlined engines has rather stolen the thunder of the 'A1s' and of the 'A3s' too, for that matter. A journey I enjoyed on the 10.5 am down Junior Scotsman in the late summer of 1937 did, however, show, better than anything I had hitherto recorded, what an 'A1' could do over the Grantham-York section. With 'A4'-hauled trains before and behind him in the morning procession from Kings Cross, the driver of 'A1' No 2581 *Neil Gow* was evidently determined to do some thunder stealing on his own account. With a gross load of 535 tons we were through Newark in exactly 15 min at 80 mph; sustained 74 across the Trent Valley right to Crow Park, and with a minimum of 56 mph at Markham and a top speed of 79 at Grove Road, passed Retford in 31 min 32 sec. Continuing in tremendous style, Black Carr Junction was passed in 44 min 13 sec, at 75 mph, after which we had to make a special stop at Doncaster. In spite of this delay, which cost us fully 10 min in running, we passed Chaloners Whin Junction in 86 min 29 sec, and would have made York in 90 min but for concluding delays. The very fast net time of 80 min from Grantham represented, however, a gain to engine of no more than 3 min on the strenuous booking then in force. Leveson, of Heaton shed, was the driver.

But of my own experiences the most impressive of all, perhaps, was a run in the autumn of 1936, when the Flying Scotsman was running to the 7¼-hr timing with a call at Newcastle. Throughout from Waverley to Kings Cross we were hauled by the historic engine of the 1925 exchange, No 4474 *Victor Wild*, with a heavy load of 475 tons. The running time then allowed was 430 min for the 392.7 miles; our gross running time was 423 min 6 sec inclusive of a permanent way slack that just about accounted for the odd 3 min, thus showing that an 'A1' could maintain the later 7-hr timing. As to the speed capabilities of these engines, I cannot do better in closing than refer to that run 'in positively heroic mould'—to quote Mr Cecil J. Allen—of the Scarborough Flyer in 1936, when Driver Duddington and No 4473 *Solario* beat the Silver Jubilee schedule between Hitchin and Selby, with a 395-ton load. On this memorable occasion the 141.2 miles from Stevenage to Templehirst, including, of course, the Peterborough slack, were covered at an average speed of 74.4 mph. Full details of this run were published in *The Railway Magazine* for September 1936.

4

The immediate post-grouping period

On 1 January 1923, the Great Northern Railway, as a separate concern, ceased to exist; but with Gresley appointed as Chief Mechanical Engineer of the newly-formed London & North Eastern Railway, a continuance of the traditions of Doncaster was assured, at a time when many famous dynasties of the locomotive world were soon to die out. In the previous chapter a considerable incursion was made into post-grouping history in order to present the whole story of the development of the 'A1' Pacifics; now, it is necessary to go back to 1923 to review some other events of the first few post-grouping years.

On the Great Northern Railway, three-cylinder propulsion had been given a fairly extended trial, and by the late summer of 1923 Gresley had twelve Pacifics at work, in addition to the '1000' class Moguls (now Class 'K3'), and the 2-8-0 mineral engines. The advantages of the three-cylinder type of locomotive were summarised by him, in a paper read before the Institution of Mechanical Engineers in May 1925 as follows:

1 Less coal consumption than with the two-cylinder type of equal power.
2 Increased mileage between general repairs.
3 Less tyre wear than with the two-cylinder type.
4 Lighter reciprocating parts can be used, consequently hammerblow on the rails is reduced, and for equal bridge stresses a greater permissible weight can be allowed on the coupled wheels of the three-cylinder type.
5 More uniform starting effort than with either the two-cylinder type or the four-cylinder with directly opposed cranks.
6 Lower permissible factor of adhesion; thus with a given weight on the coupled wheels, a higher tractive effort can be obtained without increasing the tendency to slip.
7 An earlier cut-off in full gear.

Gresley was fortunate in being able to subject the two systems of propulsion to a practical test on locomotives that were identical save in the number of cylinders. Trials were carried out in September 1924 with express trains on the Newcastle-Edinburgh road, in which a three-cylinder North Eastern Atlantic (LNER Class 'C7') proved superior to the competing two-cylinder engine of Class

'C6'; in the following February, tests with ex-GNR 2-8-0 locomotives of Classes 'O1' and 'O2' gave similar results, this time in heavy coal traffic. The published figures of the latter set of trials sum up concisely the performance of the 'O1' and 'O2' Classes, and from this data the following details have been taken, relating to the southbound run from New England yard, Peterborough, to Ferme Park:

Engine No	3466	3479
Type	2-cylinder	3-cylinder
Load behind tender, tons	1,310	1,315
Average speed (mph)	13.2	13.6
Boiler pressure (average), (lb per sq in)	163½	162½
Steam chest pressure (average), (lb per sq in)	107½	113½
Superheat temperature (average) (F)	500	531
Average cut-off, per cent	47	47
Water consumed per dhp hour (lb)	32	28.1
Coal consumed per dhp hour (lb)	5.24	4.78

It will be seen that in practically identical conditions the three-cylinder engine showed an economy over the two-cylinder of 12 per cent in water consumption, and 9 per cent in coal consumption. These results, after those obtained in the trials of the ex-NER Atlantics, did much to influence future LNER locomotive policy.

Most of the individual railways that were merged to form the LNER were, it is true, fairly well equipped for the needs of the moment, though everywhere train loads showed a tendency to rise. As far as speed was concerned train services were, with a few exceptions, stagnant. Of the nearest neighbours of the Great Northern, the Great Central and the Great Eastern sections were more than holding their own, though on the latter the haulage of the evening Continental boat expresses from Liverpool Street to Parkeston Quay, with the 350 to 400-ton loads of that period, was a task not far short of the maximum capabilities of the Holden superheater 4-6-0s, the design of which dates back to 1912. On the North Eastern the drafting of the Gresley Pacifics to the East Coast expresses released a number of Atlantics for secondary duties, and it was only on the North British that anything like an immediate problem existed in the years just after the grouping. Here the greatest need was for a locomotive of intermediate power rating. In general the Reid Atlantics were well on top of their job on the heaviest turns; but these 22 engines were rather sparsely distributed between the Aberdeen, the Perth, and the Carlisle roads, and there was a big disparity between the power developed by them and their next-of-kin, the superheated 'Scott' class 4-4-0s. The use of Pacifics was, no doubt, contemplated for the heaviest work of the future, but the immediate needs were

'Improved Director' class 4-4-0 No 6393 *The Fiery Cross* at Haymarket shed. (*O.S. Nock*)

A Crail to Glasgow stopping train at North Queensferry, the entry to the Forth bridge, hauled by 4-4-0 No 62687 *Lord James of Douglas* ('Improved Director' class) in BR livery. (*E.D. Bruton*)

pressing and allowed no time for the preparation of an entirely new design for immediate duty.

A locomotive designer faced with such a problem would naturally incline towards some type with which he was already familiar, and the sending to Scotland of the Great Northern superheater 4-4-0s of the '51-65' class, designed by Ivatt, was a logical first step. These engines, now classed 'D1', had their boiler mountings cut down to conform to the North British loading gauge, and were fitted with the Westinghouse brake. They did well in Scotland, and to outsiders it seemed that this might be the beginning of a general infiltration of Doncaster types throughout the LNER system. But, this seeming hint proved to be no hint at all, for the

new engines built for service in Scotland were of Robinson's Great Central 'Improved Director' class. This type had much to commend it, though on a tractive effort basis it is but little more powerful than the North British 'Scott' design. The cylinders were the same, 20 in diameter by 26 in stroke, and the higher boiler pressure, 180 against 165 lb per sq in, was partly counteracted by the larger coupled wheels of the Great Central engines. The boiler and firebox of the latter, however, were considerably larger, and the 26½ sq ft of grate area in the 'Directors' helped to meet the heavy but intermittent demands for steam on such routes as Edinburgh-Aberdeen and Edinburgh-Perth. The introduction of the 'Directors' to the Scottish Area exemplified the locomotive policy pursued for many years by the LNER after grouping. No attempt was made to flood the other sections with Doncaster ideas and Doncaster engines. The Great Eastern and Great Central sections remained as self-contained units, operated by few other than their own pre-grouping locomotives, and even on the North Eastern, where, owing to the through East Coast workings, more change was apparent, the Worsdell and Raven types were rarely seen outside their home ground. Furthermore, a number of years elapsed before any degree of rebuilding was applied to pre-grouping designs. The new 'Directors', 24 in all, were built, 12 each, by Kitson & Co Ltd, and Armstrong, Whitworth & Co Ltd, and delivery began in the autumn of 1924. Nos 6378-6401 originally were un-named. But the high-tide of railway publicity that gave us 'King Arthurs', Pacifics named after racehorses, and regimental and other names, saw the Scottish 'Directors' named after characters in the Waverley novels.

A Great Central engine on an East Coast express: four-cylinder 4-6-0 No 6169 *Lord Faringdon* on the Harrogate Pullman passing Belle Isle. (*Rail Archive Stephenson*)

Great Northern
Atlantics restored to the
Pullmans: engine No
4433 on the down
Queen of Scots near
Grantham. (*Rail Archive
Stephenson, T.G.
Hepburn*)

At the same time, other Great Central engines were concerned
in a long-term exchange with the Great Northern section. Upon
the introduction of the Harrogate Pullman expresses in the summer of 1923, some of the four-cylinder 4-6-0s of the 'Lord Faringdon' class were transferred to Kings Cross shed for this duty, but
these nominally powerful engines were not altogether a success.
The 'Directors' that succeeded them, working from the Leeds end,
had a much longer innings, and on the 3 hr 25 min bookings
between Kings Cross and Leeds kept time without difficulty; their
small grates told against them, however, when their coal consumption was compared with that of the Great Northern Atlantics working on the same service, and when the accelerations of 1932 came
the Atlantics were left in sole possession. But while the Great Central engines proved to be only long-term visitors to the Great
Northern section, a number of the large-boilered Ivatt Atlantics
seem to have settled down permanently at Sheffield GC shed.
Considering the formidable gradients over which engines stationed there have to work, over the Pennines to Manchester, and
southward over shorter yet little easier inclines between Sheffield
and Nottingham, the comparative smallness of their nominal tractive effort has not been a serious handicap, being so much offset
by their large free-steaming boilers and the high degree of superheat now attained as to permit of excellent hill-climbing performances.

Very soon after the grouping, Gresley used one of the large superheater GN Atlantics for the trial of a booster, converting the trailing wheels into an additional pair of drivers to provide extra power when severe conditions required it. No 1419, now LNER No 4419, was fitted with a booster engine having two cylinders 10 in diameter by 12 in stroke; this engine, acting upon the 3 ft 8 in diameter trailing wheels, provided an additional 8,500 lb of tractive effort, at 85 per cent of the working pressure of 170 lb per sq in. As the nominal tractive effort of the main engine is 17,340 lb, the booster, when in action, provided an increase of almost 50 per cent. To accommodate the auxiliary engine it was necessary to lengthen the main frames of the locomotive at the foot-plate end, and opportunity was taken to provide a much more commodious cab. Subsequently, No 4419 had her boiler mountings cut down to permit of running on the North British section. A test run made in July 1923 over heavy gradients in the London district showed the beneficial effect of the booster; a train of no less than 18 bogies was hauled up the banks with ease, and started cleanly from rest in several awkward locations. Since this initial experiment several other locomotives have been fitted with boosters, most of which have now been removed. Reference will be made later to these.

In the middle 1920s, when all this interesting passenger engine activity was manifest, little of a corresponding kind was happen-

The Queen of Scots north of Edinburgh, approaching Waverley station, hauled by North British Atlantic No 9877 *Liddesdale*. (*Author's collection*)

The booster-fitted GNR Atlantic No 4419 at Grantham in 1930. (*Rail Archive Stephenson, T.G. Hepburn*)

ing in the LNER freight locomotive realm. Having regard to the company's vast mineral traffic it is remarkable that, with the exception of the two Class 'P1' Mikado engines of 1925, not a single new design for the heaviest freight service has been turned out since the grouping took place. This may be taken as a compliment to the capacity of the Great Northern and Great Central Consolidations, and to the several varieties of North Eastern 0-8-0; like the pre-grouping passenger types, these engines are still confined almost exclusively to their original sections. In 1931-2, however, when more locomotives were required for the Great Eastern section, a new series of Great Northern 'O2' three-cylinder 2-8-0s were built specially, and ex-ROD 2-8-0s of the Great Central type (LNER Class 'O4') are to be found in varying numbers over the whole system.

The Gresley Mikados of 1925 were a natural development of the Pacific type for heavy mineral service. They were experimental, not in the locomotive sense but from the operating point of view; it is, indeed, a moot point whether trains of the immense length hauled by Nos 2393 and 2394 are an economical proposition having regard to siding, refuge loop and yard capacity. Loads of 1,600 tons held no terrors for these capable engines, and special paths had to be arranged in the working timetables for the 100-wagon coal trains that they were rostered to work from Peterborough to Ferme Park. From all accounts, however, the Midados seem, originally, to have been something of a problem to fire. The boiler was the same as that fitted to the 'A1' Pacifics, but though the cylinders were also the same, the valve gear was modified to give 75 per cent cut-off in full gear, against 65 per cent in the 'A1' engines.

The coupled wheels were 5 ft 2 in diameter, and the nominal tractive effort, at 85 per cent of the 180 lb boiler pressure, 38,500 lb. To assist in the haulage of heavy loads on the long 1 in 200 gradients a booster was fitted to the trailing axle. This auxiliary engine had two cylinders 10 in diameter by 12 in stroke, and provided an additional 9,000 lb of tractive effort when it was in action; it was thus identical in size with that fitted to the Atlantic engine No 4419, though on account of the higher boiler pressure of the Mikados, slightly more powerful. One of the most interesting exploits of No 2394 took place when the design for the express passenger Mikados was in contemplation. As a test she was put on to the 7.45 am semifast train from Kings Cross, and attained speeds of up to 65 mph on the run to Peterborough.

The first of the Mikados, No 2393, was completed in time to take part in the Railway Centenary celebrations at Darlington in 1925.

Ex-Great Central 2-8-0 No 6238 on a down GN line freight near Retford. (*P. Ransome Wallis*)

Gresley's first 2-8-2 three-cylinder heavy mineral engine, No 2393, with booster. (*British Railways*)

Three-cylinder 2-8-2 engine No 2393 hauling a 100-wagon loaded coal train near Potters Bar. (*F.R. Hebron*)

With her was exhibited another remarkable Gresley locomotive, the one and only LNER 'Garratt', which had been completed by Beyer, Peacock & Co Ltd about the same time. This engine was designed specially for banking duties, and her machinery is the equivalent of two Class 'O2' 2-8-0 tender engines, the wheels, cylinders and motion being interchangeable. The boiler has all the 'Garratt' characteristics, short length, big diameter and large tubes; the barrel, though 7 ft diameter, is only 13 ft between the tube plates, and the grate area is no less than 56.4 sq ft. The total heating surface is 3,640 sq ft, of which the superheater provides 646 sq ft. The nominal tractive effort of this notable engine is 72,940 lb, the largest of any British type. Although designed for short hauls, she carries 7 tons of coal and 5,000 gallons of water. No 2395 is employed purely as a banking engine, at Wentworth, on

The second 2-8-2 engine, No 2394, with modified superheater. (*British Railways*)

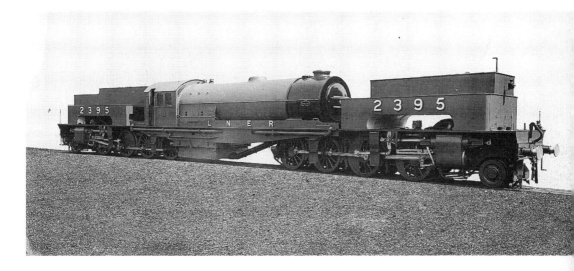

the line between Wath marshalling yard and Penistone; the line is used only by mineral trains and avoids Barnsley altogether.

The actual method of working the very heavy coal trains is interesting. The maximum load of westbound trains is 63 wagons, about 1,000 tons loaded, and for this two Class 'O4' ex-GCR 2-8-0s are used. The trains are double-headed from Wath to Wombwell, but at the latter point a stop is made, and the assistant engine is transferred from front to rear of the train; thus they continue to Wentworth, where the worst gradient begins. From Wentworth the 'Garratt' assists in rear up the 1 in 40 gradient, there thus being one 'O4' at the front of the train, and one 'O4' and the 'Garratt' in rear. The distance usually assisted is about 2½ miles, and on arrival at West Silkstone Junction, where this goods avoiding line joins the Barnsley-Penistone line, the 'Garratt' comes off. She then

The giant six-cylinder Garratt for working on the Worsborough Incline. (*Beyer Peacock & Co*)

Class 'O2' three-cylinder 2-8-0 engine No 3482 on a down goods train near Hatfield. (*G.R. Grigs*)

returns light to Wentworth, to assist another train. She manages about 18 banking trips in the 24 hours.

Towards the end of 1924 further multiplication of the '1000' class Moguls began. A batch of 50 locomotives was turned out from Darlington works differing only in certain details, including the boiler mountings, from the original examples, and with typically North Eastern cabs. Hitherto the '1000s' or 'K3s', as they are now classified, had appeared on passenger trains to only a small extent; but they were fast engines, capable of speeds up to 75 mph, and as more became available they were frequently requisitioned for intermediate workings all over the system. After a week's strenuous going on fitted freight trains, their weekend respite often took the form of a trip with a half-day excursion train. It is a striking commentary on their tractive powers that in pre-war days with the most famous of all the fast goods trains, the 3.35 pm Scotsman, they were rostered to take a maximum of 55 wagons on the 111¾-mile non-stop run from Peterborough to York. The booked average speed is 45 mph, and the gross load may rise to 650 tons behind the tender.

I had a fine trip on the footplate of No 2450 on this service, details of which are given in the accompanying table.

Sometimes, if the arrival from London has been exceptionally early, it is despatched about 6.15 pm, and then turned slow road from Essendine to Stoke to let the Jubilee go by, but on my trip we ran in the normal path. This was fortunate, as the 40-min timing from Westwood to passing Grantham is one of the most strenuous goods train bookings to be found anywhere in the country. There must be a strong temptation to drop a little time on this section, for it is succeeded by the much easier one of 43 min for the 33.1 miles from Grantham to Retford. But Driver Sallins opened No 2450 out to some purpose, made a splendid ascent and kept time.

Full regulator and early cut-off were again the order of the day. Sallins linked up quickly to 20 per cent cut-off and let the engine find her own stride. We topped the 50 line at Tallington, and it was not until we were well beyond Essendine that an advance in cut-off was made; then it was adjusted by 2 and 3 per cent at a time to a maximum of 28 per cent, and this by no means strenuous working took us over Stoke summit at a minimum speed of 41 mph, which was no better than the booking demands. All the way up boiler pressure was maintained at 175-177 lb per sq in and the steam chest pressure was 170 lb. At Stoke summit Sallins linked up to 15 per cent cut-off; and down the 1 in 200 with no more than 140 lb in the steamchest, we accelerated rapidly to 65 mph. North of Grantham the engine was eased; with steam chest pressure down to 110 lb speed gradually dwindled to 48½ mph by the time we passed Newark.

LNER Peterborough-York: 6.37 pm Scotch Express Goods

Engine: Class 'K3' 2-6-0 No 2450
Load: 46 wagons and brake van, 610 tons full
Driver Sallins; Fireman Truss (New England Shed)

Dist (miles)		Schedule (min)	Actual (min sec)	Speeds (mph)	Regu-later	Cut-off (per cent)	Pressure (lb per sq in)	
							Boiler	Steam chest
0.0	PETERBOROUGH	0	0 00	—	Full	65	160	150
	(Westwood Yard)		Sigs					
0.7	New England N Box		4 03	—	Full	40	—	—
2.4	Werrington Jc		6 40	42½	Full	20	180	175
7.7	Tallington		13 26	51½	Full	20		
11.5	ESSENDINE		18 10	48	Full	25	180	175
15.1	Little Bytham		23 01	43½	Full	28	180	175
18.9	Milepost 96		28 34	41	Full	28		
20.0	Corby		30 10	44	Full	28	175	170
23.0	Stoke Box		34 30	41	½	20	175	120
28.4	GRANTHAM	40	40 33	65	⅓	15	175	120
		—	easy	51	⅓	15		
43.0	NEWARK	58	56 50	48	Full	20	175	170
50.3	Crow Park		65 33	56	Full	20		
54.8	Tuxford		71 52	35½	Full	20	180	175
			Sigs	15	—	25		
56.6	Markham Box		75 53	—	—	20		
			Sigs, sev	—	—	—		
61.5	RETFORD	83	84 40	10	Full	22	160	155
66.8	Ranskill		93 14	52	Full	15	175	170
72.4	Milepost 149½		100 28	40½	¾	15	175	150
76.1	Black Carr Jc		104 57	59½	⅖	15	180	110
78.9	DONCASTER	104	108 30	46	Full	20	170	165
83.1	Shaftholme Jc		113 39	52	Full	20	177	170
88.9	Balne		120 20	54	Full	20	180	172
95.9	Brayton Jc		128 35	56	Shut	20	—	—
97.3	SELBY	127	130 30	30*	Full	32	—	—
101.4	Riccall		137 46	46	Full	22	175	170
109.1	Chaloners Whin Jc		147 14	51½	Full	22		
111.8	YORK (Severus Jc)	149	153 25‡	—	—	—		

* Severe service slack   ‡ Net time 147 min

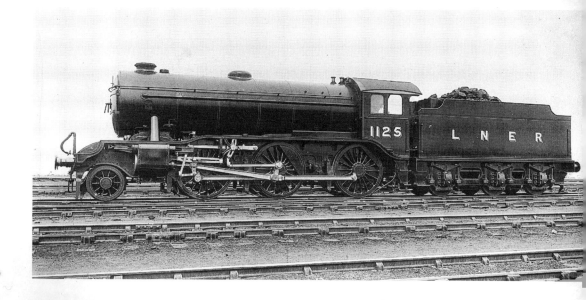

One of the later standard Class 'K3' 2-6-0s, No 1125, in the black livery. (*British Railways*)

From here it is reasonably hard going right on to York. On full regulator and 20 per cent cut-off we picked up in fine style across the level of the Trent Valley, but then unfortunately, just as we were getting some time in hand to offset the difficulty of the concluding point-to-point times, there came a string of signal checks culminating in a virtual stop at Retford South. 'Some bit of a passenger train in the way,' remarked the driver. In getting off again No 2450 was linked up to 15 per cent as early as Retford Canal box; we were running at 59½ mph approaching Black Carr Junction, and after easing to 46 through Doncaster settled down to a hard spell on full regulator and 20 per cent cut-off along the faintly adverse length to Selby. The top speed here was 56 mph. But only one minute of the six lost at Retford was regained, and this was lost again on the tightly-timed last lap, which is 22 min from passing Selby to the stop at Severus Junction—a stiff booking considering that a train like the 1.20 pm Scotsman is allowed 17 min into York station, a run 2 to 2½ min easier. The slightly adverse nature of the road on this section tells heavily with such a train, and in spite of using 22 per cent cut-off instead of the usual 20 on the level, we did not get above 50½ mph. So we were 3½ min late on arrival; but our net time was only 147 minutes, a fine average of 45½ mph with such a load.

Equally the haulage of 400-ton express passenger trains has presented little trouble, and the 'K3s' have done excellent work in particular with the London-Leeds expresses over the heavy grades of the West Riding, where maximum speeds up to 79 mph have been recorded with them. Fine running was regularly made on the Sunday excursions from London, as when Mr L.J. Burley timed No 2427, with a 15-car train of 500 tons gross, over the 73.9 miles from Peterborough to Finsbury Park in 81 min or 78 min net. Indeed, the 'K3s' are second to none among main-line mixed-traffic locomotives, and the only drawback to their universal employment on the system is the heavy loading of 20 tons on each of the coupled axles, which precludes their use over much of the Great Eastern section.

Two new designs of 0-6-0 goods engine for secondary services came out in 1926, of similar dimensions except wheel diameter; one, classed 'J38', had 4 ft 8 in diameter wheels, and the others, the 'J39' class, had 5 ft 2 in wheels. The cylinders were 20 in by 26 in. The boiler was a new and enlarged design, with excellent steaming qualities. The firebox is long and deep, having a grate area of 26 sq ft, and the boiler barrel, 10 ft 9 in between the tube plates, is short in proportion to its large diameter of 5 ft 6 in. The total evaporative heating surface is 1,398 sq ft. The 24-element superheater is on the small side for a Gresley locomotive, affording only 246 sq ft of heating surface, but both the 'J38' and 'J39' classes are intended for short hauls rather than long through runs

of many hours' duration, and under such conditions the advantages to be gained from high superheat would be small. The working pressure is 180 lb per sq in. Since their introduction the 'J39s' have multiplied exceedingly and now number 271 engines, while there are 35 'J38s' at work. The latter are all employed in Scotland, and the former principally in England. The 'J39s' have a good turn of speed, and are often to be seen on passenger trains.

A standard 'J39' Class 0-6-0 No 1856, one of a large batch built by Beyer Peacock & Co in 1936. (*Beyer Peacock & Co*)

5

New express passenger types, 1926-30

In September 1927, the first of the new intermediate class of express passenger locomotives was turned out from Darlington works, 4-4-0 No 234 *Yorkshire*. Hitherto Gresley had confined the three-cylinder system of propulsion to locomotives intended for the heaviest duties, but this 4-4-0 design marked the beginning of its almost universal adoption on the LNER for new classes. The new 4-4-0s were classed 'D49', but as their names are those of counties served by the LNER they have always been referred to as the 'Shires'. In them the three cylinders drive on to the leading pair of coupled wheels, and the absence of a coupled axle ahead of the driving axle enables all three cylinders to be set in line, and the three cranks exactly at 120 degrees to each other. In this respect the 'Shires' differ from the Pacifics and the 'K3' Moguls. The valve-gear is also simplified, by having the rocking levers that operate the valve-spindle of the inside cylinder behind the cylinders, instead of in front. This arrangement eliminates the factor of expansion of the valve-spindles, which has to be taken into account in the gear fitted to the Pacifics and the 'K3s'. The maximum travel of the valves is greater than that of the 'A1' Pacifics—6 in against 5¾ in—and a further important factor towards a free-running engine is the size of the piston-valves in proportion to the cylinders; the valves of the 'Shires' are 8 in diameter as in the Pacifics, whereas the 'Shire' cylinders are only 17 in diameter. The coupled wheels are 6 ft 8 in diameter, and the weight of the engine in working order is 66 tons, of which 42 tons are available for adhesion.

The nominal tractive effort of 21,556 lb (at 85 per cent of the working pressure) makes the 'Shires' almost equal in power to any of the Atlantics built by the constituent companies of the LNER. The boiler is the same as that used on the 'J39' 0-6-0 goods engines, and alongside those of the Ivatt, Raven and Reid Atlantics its total heating surface of 1,669 sq ft seems small; but in conjunction with the customary short cut-off working there never seems to be any difficulty in providing steam for the most arduous duties. A striking example of their capacity for heavy load haulage was given by a run described in the April 1933 instalment of 'British Locomotive Practice and Performance', wherein the pioneer engine No 234 *Yorkshire* worked a load of 480 tons gross

over the 44.1 miles from Darlington to York in 48 min 41 sec, a start-to-stop average of 54.2 mph. In the North Eastern Area, however, their duties were not usually so heavy; they were put to work mostly on services radiating from Leeds, Hull and Sheffield, their most important turn being the morning Leeds to Glasgow luncheon car express, from Leeds to Newcastle. In the Scottish Area their work was harder. On all routes, at first, they took loads up to the maximum handled by the North British Atlantics, and I have seen them pounding away on the Aberdeen road with 380-390-ton gross loads, doing well too. The best performance that I have ever known with a 'Shire' was on the 1.20 pm down Scotsman, when No 249 *Aberdeenshire* had to take a 435-ton train from Newcastle to Edinburgh without assistance.

Class 'D49' three-cylinder 4-4-0 No 264 *Stirlingshire* at Tweedmouth shed. (*O.S. Nock*)

Class 'D49' three-cylinder 4-4-0 No 2753 *Cheshire*. (*British Railways*)

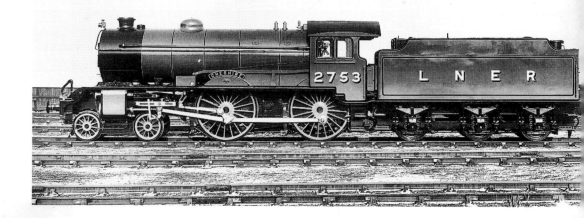

Class 'D49' 4-4-0
No 62702 *Oxfordshire*
passing through Princes
Street Gardens,
Edinburgh, with the
10.50 am stopping train
to Thornton Junction.
(*E.D. Bruton*)

The train was running in two portions on this occasion. How the relief section was loaded I do not know, but the main train brought 16 vehicles down from London, with the then usual three in front and three on the rear to be detached at Newcastle. Ten coaches would not have been too stiff a job for a 'D49', but on arrival at Newcastle it was found that more accommodation was needed; and so it was decided to send the three front coaches forward to Edinburgh. The task set to No 249 *Aberdeenshire* thus became a formidable one, particularly as the conditional stops at both Dunbar and Drem were to be made. Under these conditions it was inevitable that time would be lost, but the actual work of the locomotive was magnificent, and allowing for the stops at Alnmouth, Dunbar and Drem the equivalent non-stop times work out at 75 minutes from Newcastle to Berwick, and 66½ minutes from Berwick to Edinburgh. The going was good enough from Morpeth to Alnmouth, with an average of 62.3 mph from Pegswood to Warkworth, and better still on to Berwick, where we did some really fast running along the coast. But easily the finest feat of the trip, and incidentally one of the finest pieces of 4-4-0 hill-climbing I have ever seen, was the maintenance of a minimum speed of 46½ mph up the 1 in 200 to Grantshouse. This involved an output of about 1,230 dhp, an exceptional figure for a 4-4-0 locomotive. This performance was indeed exceptional in every way, for it rarely happened that the 'D49s' were set so strenuous a task.

The steady trend of development in locomotive engineering

LNER Newcastle-Edinburgh

Engine: 3-cylinder 4-4-0 No 249 *Aberdeenshire*
Load: 13 cars, 412 tons tare, 435 tons gross
Driver: McKillop (Haymarket Shed)

Dist. (miles)		Schedule (min)	Actual (min sec)	Speeds (mph)
0.0	NEWCASTLE	0	0 00	—
1.7	Heaton	—	4 26	—
5.0	Forest Hall	—	10 03	37
9.9	Cramlington	—	16 22	53-48
13.9	Stannington	—	20 33	66
16.6	MORPETH*	22½	23 35	*35
18.5	Pegswood	—	26 05	56
23.2	Widdrington	—	30 43	64½-58½
28.5	Acklington	—	35 49	61½-67½
31.9	Warkworth	—	39 00	62
34.8	ALNMOUTH	41	43 10	
2.7	Longhoughton	—	5 59	34
4.6	Little Mill	—	9 17	36
8.2	Christon Bank	—	13 27	65
11.2	Chathill	—	16 09	69
16.8	Belford	20½	21 19	63½
23.8	Beal	—	27 19	76½
28.7	Scremerston	—	31 43	58½
30.9	Tweedmouth*	—	34 15	†54
32.1	BERWICK	36	36 22	—
1.1	*Marshall Meadows*	3	3 30	30
5.6	Burnmouth	—	11 18	37½
11.2	Reston Junction	14	17 24	§62½
16.3	Grantshouse	19	23 32	46½
21.0	Cockburnspath	—	28 07	75
26.2	Oxwellmains	—	32 14	Π80½
28.4	DUNBAR	¶33	35 55	—
5.7	East Linton	—	9 02	50½
8.3	East Fortune	—	11 45	†64½
11.3	DREM	††12	15 32	—
4.6	Longniddry Junction	††5	7 54	60
8.3	Prestonpans	—	11 45	57-62½
11.3	Inveresk	—	14 34	66½
14.8	Portobello*	††16	19 12	—
17.8	EDINBURGH	‡‡22	24 37	

* Service slack   † On shutting off steam   ‡ At top of 1 in 190   § At milepost 48½
Π At Innerwick   ¶ Start to pass   †† Pass to pass   ‡‡ Pass to stop

practice that has been so marked a feature of the Gresley régime was at a very interesting stage in the years 1927 and '28. Long-lap valves had been tried, and eventually standardised, and next there came a series of experiments leading to the adoption of higher boiler pressures. These tests were also carried out on Pacific engines. In July 1927 one of the original batch of 'A1s', No 4480 *Enterprise*, was put into traffic fitted with a new boiler having a working pressure of 220 lb per sq in. The object was to obtain costs of maintenance, and comparative data as to the life of fireboxes, stays and tubes, between boilers carrying 180 lb and 220 lb pressure. The superheater was enlarged from 32 to 43 elements,

the corresponding increase in heating surface being from 525 to
706 sq ft, and the higher pressure raised the nominal tractive effort
from the 29,835 lb of the standard Pacifics to 36,465 lb. The heavier
boiler, and a small redistribution of weight elsewhere, increased
the adhesion from 60 to 66 tons.

Enterprise was, of course, fitted with long-lap valves at the time
of her rebuilding, and in traffic she displayed an easy mastery over
any regular task existing on the Southern Area main line at that
time. In some ways she was too powerful, for even when fully
linked up, to 15 per cent, it was not possible to use full regulator
without making extravagant gains on schedule time. To investigate
further the advantages to be gained from the use of higher steam
pressures, another of the 'A1s', No 2544 *Lemberg*, was fitted with
a boiler similar to that of No 4480, but the cylinders were lined
up to 18¼-in diameter, thus giving this high-pressure engine a
nominal tractive effort equal to that of the standard 180 lb Pacifics.

A series of dynamometer-car trials were then conducted, in
February 1928, between *Lemberg* and No 4473 *Solario*, a standard
'A1' fitted with long-lap valves. At that time the expresses between
London and the West Riding provided the hardest daily tasks set
to the Pacifics, and the trials were conducted on the 10.51 am from
Doncaster to Kings Cross, and the regular return working, the
4 pm down. The published results of two weeks' running showed
no appreciable difference between the two locomotives. The average coal consumption was 3.08 lb per drawbar horsepower hour
by *Solario* and 3.12 lb by *Lemberg*. The latter engine enjoyed better
weather during her week, and on that account her coal consumption per train-mile was less than that of her rival—35.37 against
38.83 lb. Both, however, were excellent figures, considering that
the average train loads were 431 tons from Doncaster to Kings
Cross, 498 tons from Kings Cross to Peterborough and 339 tons
thence to Doncaster.

In ordinary service *Lemberg* earned the reputation of being one
of the speediest of all the non-streamlined Pacifics. After the
accelerations of 1932 she often worked the 8.40 am from Doncaster
to Kings Cross, and with her regular driver, Charlie Molson, of
Doncaster shed, one could always look forward to some sparkling
performance on the 63.4 mph run from Grantham to Kings Cross.
One of the finest of such feats was timed by Mr R.A.H. Weight,
on a day when an unusually heavy load for that train was carried,
435 tons gross. A number of delays prevented strict time-keeping,
but intermediately there was some grand going, including the high
maximum, for 1933, of 92½ mph, at Essendine. The net time was
97 min, a start-to-stop average of 65.3 mph. In the same summer
she worked the Scarborough Flyer, loaded to no less than 570 tons
gross, non-stop from Kings Cross to York, 188.2 miles in 192½ min
net. In view of these splendid performances it is perhaps signi-

ficant that the steam port area of this engine is larger, in proportion to the total cylinder volume, than in any other of the non-streamlined Pacifics; for when the cylinders were lined up to 18¼ in diameter the original 8 in diameter valves were retained. This feature of her design would certainly help in giving that freedom of exhaust that is so essential for fast and efficient running.

From the data provided from the experimental rebuilding of engines 4480 and 2544, the new so-called Super-Pacific design, Class 'A3', was prepared. No 2743 *Felstead*, the first of a batch of ten locomotives, was put into service in August 1928; in these the boiler was identical with that of *Lemberg*, but though the cylinders were increased to 19 in diameter the 8 in diameter piston-valves, common to all previous Pacifics, were retained. The nominal tractive effort at 85 per cent boiler pressure was 32,909 lb. Class 'A3' is being increased by conversions from Class 'A1', apart from the two experimental engines, 2544 and 4480. Soon after the rebuilding of 4480 three others were similarly altered, namely Nos 2573 *Harvester*, 2578 *Bayardo* and 2580 *Shotover*, and others have been converted since the outbreak of war. The last engines built new as Class 'A3' were a batch of nine—Nos 2500-8, turned out in 1934-5, which have the modified dome arrangement including a perforated steam collector.

As to 'A3' performance, the test runs of No 2750 *Papyrus* on 5 March 1935 rank high among the classics of British locomotive running and are assured of fame equal to that enjoyed by those almost legendary feats of former days, such as the GWR Ocean Mail run of 9 May 1904, and of the rival Scotch racing trains on the night of 22 August 1895. But the subsequent progress in railway speed was such that the record times of *Papyrus* were to become almost a commonplace in the years 1936-9 in the day-to-day running of the streamlined trains. With the 'A4' Pacifics this is understandable, but occasions like those of the week ending 25 March 1939 leave one rather at a loss for words. Twice in this one week 'A3s' had to take on at short notice the haulage of the up Coronation between Newcastle and Kings Cross, and twice in this one week the record of *Papyrus* was surpassed, with 290-ton loads against the 217 tons of the test run. It is a thousand pities that no more detailed records than those of the guard's journals are available, but enough is known to establish them firmly among the finest feats ever achieved by 'A3' Pacifics. On the first occasion the train arrived punctually and the defect in the booked engine was only discovered when the driver climbed down to give the usual short examination. No 2595 *Trigo* was commandeered on the spot. Although leaving Newcastle 8 minutes late the train was on time by Retford, having covered the 129.7 miles in 120½ min. Onwards to London only a single minute was dropped, in spite of about 5 min loss in running through a couple of pw slacks.

Class 'A3' 4-6-2 No 2744 *Grand Parade* passing through York with the up non-stop Flying Scotsman. (*Rail Archive Stephenson, T.G. Hepburn*)

First of the final batch of 'A3' 4-6-2s, No 2500 *Windsor Lad*. (*British Railways*)

The net time from Newcastle was approximately 225 min, an average of 71¾ mph. Two days later, when the circumstances were to a large extent repeated, No 2507 *Singapore* was the engine, with the same crew as before, Driver Nash and Fireman Gilbey of Kings Cross. They were 34 min late away from Newcastle, but 8½ min had been regained by Doncaster. The same relaying slacks as before were experienced, but despite the additional hindrance of a signal check at Bawtry no more time was lost, and Kings Cross was reached in 227½ min from Newcastle. Comparison of the journal times on the delayed sections with normal runs suggests that at least 5 min was lost by these delays, giving the record net time of 222½ min, an average of 72¼ mph. The time of *Papyrus*, with 217 tons, was 227½ min net.

As to heavy load haulage, No 2744 *Grand Parade* still holds the

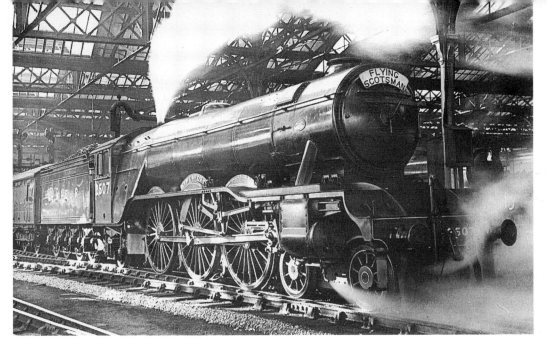

record for the fastest time ever made from Kings Cross to passing Peterborough with a load of over 500 tons. I was lucky enough to be a passenger on the 1.20 pm Scotsman on this occasion and noted the remarkable time of 73 min 55 sec for this distance of 76.4 miles. With 530 tons behind the tender we passed Hatfield in 24 min 40 sec, and then put on a terrific spurt, for those days, averaging 77.8 mph from Hitchin to Huntingdon. The maximum was 87½ mph. This was at Whitsun, 1932. Then on my very last trip over the East Coast route before the outbreak of the war, No 2507 *Singapore* was responsible for some further mighty weight-pulling on the 4.27 pm (Saturdays) non-stop express from York to Kings Cross. The log overleaf gives summarised details of our progress, but to my mind the outstanding feature of the run lay in the steady maintenance of 74-75 mph on the level road between

Class 'A3' 4-6-2 No 2507 *Singapore* on the down Flying Scotsman in Newcastle Central. (*W.B. Greenfield*)

A down East Coast express near Plessey hauled by 'A3' 4-6-2 No 2508 *Brown Jack*. (*Norman Wilkinson*)

LNER 4.27 pm York-Kings Cross

Engine: 'A3' 4-6-2 No 2507 *Singapore*
Load: 15 coaches, 504 tons tare, 540 tons full
Driver Hunt: Fireman Cook (Kings Cross Shed)

Dist (miles)		Schedule (min)	Actual (min sec)	Speeds (mph)
0.0	YORK	0	0 00	
4.2	Naburn		6 32	57½
9.7	Riccall		11 40	72
			Sigs	30
13.8	SELBY	18	17 38	25*
18.4	Templehirst		23 30	61
28.0	Shaftholme Junction		31 53	74/75
—			Sigs	30
32.2	DONCASTER	38	36 37	—
35.0	Black Carr Junction		40 00	61/55½
42.4	Scrooby		47 07	73
49.6	RETFORD	54½	54 23	51*
54.5	Markham Summit		60 24	47
60.8	Crow Park		66 00	82
68.1	NEWARK	72½	72 53	53/64½
			Sigs	25
78.5	Barkston		84 13	—
82.7	GRANTHAM	88½	90 48	52
88.1	Stoke Box		97 39	43
99.6	Essendine		107 33	86½
108.7	Werrington Junction		114 45	—
111.8	PETERBOROUGH	117½	119 00	20*
115.6	Yaxley		124 08	60
118.8	Holme		127 04	72½
124.7	Abbotts Ripton		132 28	56
129.3	HUNTINGDON	136½	136 47	78
144.1	Sandy		149 02	72
156.3	HITCHIN	161½	160 13	56
159.6	Stevenage		164 14	46
170.5	HATFIELD	177½	175 22	74½
175.5	Potters Bar		180 16	55½
183.2	Wood Green		187 29	69
185.6	Finsbury Park		189 58	—
			Sigs	
188.2	KINGS CROSS	198	195 21	

* Net time 190 minutes

Selby and Doncaster. This involved an output of about 1,600 draw-bar horsepower. Lastly, as indicating some of their work in Scotland, I have tabulated opposite the performance of No 2500 *Windsor Lad*, on the up Aberdonian sleeping car express—a performance that I was privileged to record from the footplate.

While the Super-Pacific design was being developed, a still larger engine was under construction at Darlington, the four-cylinder compound 4-6-4 No 10000. The first appearance of this unique locomotive at the close of 1929, little more than a year after the 'A3s' had come out, may have given rise to ideas that the two designs were in some way connected: that the trial of 450 lb per sq in pressure in No 10000 was a sequel to the success of the pre-

LNER 9.27 pm Dundee-Edinburgh

Engine: Class 'A3' 4-6-2 No 2500 *Windsor Lad*
Load: 414 tons tare, 440 tons full
Driver Douglas; Fireman Hood (Haymarket Shed)

Dist. (miles)		Schedule (min)	Actual (min sec)	Speeds (mph)	Regu-later	Cut-off (per cent)	Pressure (lb per sq in)	
							Boiler	Steam chest
0.0	DUNDEE	0	0 00	—	Full	65	200	190
0.8	Esplanade		3 12	—	Full	40	190	175
2.7	Tay Bridge S Jc	8	7 44	—	Full	20	200	190
8.3	LEUCHARS Jc	14	13 53	63½*	Shut	25	—	—
				50	Full	20	190	180
14.6	Cupar		20 27	63½	Full	20		
16.9	Springfield		23 00	49½	Full	20		
20.1	LADYBANK Jc	29	26 28	57½‡	Full	25	190	180
21.0	Kingskettle		27 22	62	Full	25	200	190
24.3	Lochmuir Box		31 52	31½	½	20	200	120
—			—	57½	Shut	20		
—			pws	—				
28.5	THORNTON Jc	41	37 50	15	Full	30	200	185
31.2	Dysart		43 35	27½	Full	20		
—			—	57	Shut	20		
—			pws	—				
33.3	KIRKCALDY		46 45	15	Full	25	220	205
—			—	54½	Shut	25		
36.5	Kinghorn		51 02	24	Full	25		
—			—	50	Shut			
39.1	BURNTISLAND	55	55 10	24	Full	30		
—			—	44¶	Full	30		
41.8	Aberdour		59 40	36½	Full	30		
43.1	Dalgetty Box		62 05	31½	½	20	205	195
—			—	57½	Shut	20		
46.2	INVERKEITHING	65	66 03	25¶	Full	40		
47.9	North Queensferry	70	70 35	17½	Full	40	205	195
49.7	Dalmeny	73	74 20	41	Full	20		
52.7	Turnhouse		77 33	69	Full	20		
55.8	Saughton Jc		80 33	57½/62	Full	20		
59.2	EDINBURGH	85	85 43†	—				

* Eased to 55 through station ¶ Severe service check
‡ Eased to 53 through station † Net time 80½ min

vious moderate increase, from the 180 lb of the 'A1s' to the 220 lb of the 'A3s'. Actually, however, the conception of a high-pressure locomotive design dates back almost to pre-grouping days, and was unaffected by any current events on the LNER. In a paper read before the Institution of Mechanical Engineers on 23 January 1931, Gresley tells that he was so impressed by the striking increases in efficiency obtained in land and marine boilers by the use of high steam pressures that he began to formulate a design of locomotive which it was hoped would realise the same advantages. By 1924 his own ideas were sufficiently advanced for him, in September of that year, to approach Mr Harold Yarrow, of Glasgow, with a view to the latter's firm building a high-pressure boiler of the water-tube type suitable for a locomotive. It is striking evidence of the amount of painstaking work put into the design of engine No 10000 that nearly three years were spent in preparing the design of the boiler alone; and that although the order for

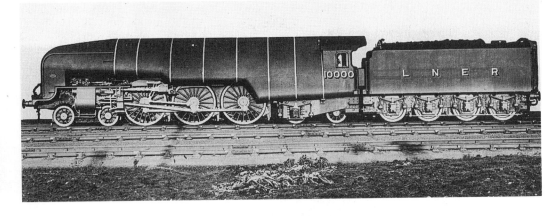

The 'hush-hush' engine: Gresley's high-pressure four-cylinder compound No 10000. (*British Railways*)

the boiler was placed with Yarrow early in 1928, it was not completed until October 1929. The engine ran its trial trip on 12 December 1929.

The working pressure was 450 lb per sq in, and to obtain the greatest possible range of expansion the engine was arranged as a compound having two high-pressure cylinders 12 in diameter and two low-pressure 20 in diameter, all four cylinders having 26 in stroke. On trial it was found that a more equal distribution of the work between the high- and low-pressure cylinders was obtained by reducing the diameter of the high-pressure cylinders to 10 in. Although using only two sets of valve-gear, Gresley introduced an arrangement making it possible to vary the cut-off in the high-pressure cylinders independently of that in the low-pressure; the advantages of having this provision will be manifest to anyone who has studied the working of the de Glehn com-

The high-pressure compound No 10000 entering Kings Cross on an up express. (*W.J. Reynolds*)

Front-end view of No 10000, incidentally displaying Royal Train headlamps! (*British Railways*)

pounds in France. The details of this gear were fully described by Gresley in the paper previously referred to. The paper itself, and the subsequent discussion, covers no less than 106 pages, and is a document of absorbing interest. The aerodynamic screening at the front end attracted a lot of attention at the time, and its unconventional appearance prepared us for *Cock o' the North* four years later.

In his paper Gresley was able to report that No 10000 'has worked trains of over 500 tons weight for long distances at express speeds with consistent success and reliability, and although it has not been possible so far to carry out any extensive trials, there is every indication that it will prove more economical in fuel consumption than express engines of the latest normal types.' During the summer of 1930 she was working in the ordinary Gateshead Pacific link, including the long-mileage double-manned turn, beginning with the 11.17 am from Newcastle to Edinburgh; this

No 10000 on her one and only trip on the down Flying Scotsman near Hadley Wood. (*A.L.P. Reavil*)

One of the first batch of 'Sandringham' class three-cylinder 4-6-0s No 2808 *Gunton*. (*W.J. Reynolds*)

latter included the 43-minute Darlington-York run of the evening Glasgow-Leeds dining car express. Mr R.A.H. Weight timed her from Darlington to York, 44.1 miles, at exactly 60 mph from start to stop with a load of 440 tons. On 31 July 1930, she worked the Flying Scotsman non-stop from Edinburgh to Kings Cross, returning on the corresponding train next day; I witnessed her arrival on the up journey, dead on time. In general performance, however, the early promise of success was not realised, and No 10000 proved a troublesome engine to maintain; but although posterity will remember her best in her rebuilt form as a giant in the noble regiment of blue streamliners, the boldness of the original conception, and the superb engineering put into her construction, must not be lightly dismissed.

The success attending the moderate advance in steam pressure

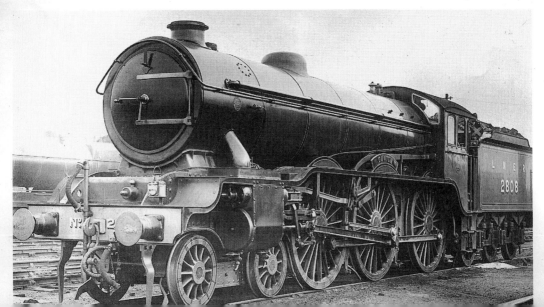

from the 170-180 lb per sq in of the earlier Gresley designs to the 220 lb of the 'A3s' resulted in the general adoption of higher pressures for future designs. The first example of this development was to be seen in the 'Sandringham' class of three-cylinder 4-6-0s, LNER class 'B17'. For some time there had been a growing need for a more powerful type of locomotive on the Great Eastern section, though the limitation of both axle loading and overall length did not appear to offer much chance of an easy solution to the problem. Happily the findings of the Bridge Stress Committee had shown that axle-loading was not the sole criterion of the effect a locomotive has upon the road, and through better balancing, and the reduction of hammer-blow due to three-cylinder propulsion, it was found possible to increase the adhesion weight from the 44 tons of the Holden 4-6-0s to 54 tons in the 'Sandringhams'. The engine layout differs from every other Gresley three-cylinder type, in that the drive is divided; the outside cylinders drive on the middle pair of coupled wheels and the inside cylinder drives on to the leading pair. The principal dimensions are: cylinders, three, 17½-in diameter by 26-in stroke; piston valves 8-in diameter with a travel, in full gear, of $5^{21}/_{32}$in; boiler, 5 ft 6 in maximum outside diameter, 14 ft 0 in between the tube-plates, and having tubes of the ample diameter, for their length, of 2 in; superheater, 24 element, affording 344 sq ft of heating surface; total heating surface 2,020 sq ft; grate area 27½ sq ft; working pressure 200 lb per sq in. As usual in Gresley express locomotives the coupled wheels are 6 ft 8 in diameter. Although the preparation of the design was beset with many difficulties, imposed by the nature of the Great Eastern road, a most successful engine was produced, the nominal tractive effort of which, 25,380 lb, represented a substantial advance upon the 21,969 lb

'Sandringham' class three-cylinder 4-6-0 No 2822 *Alnwick Castle* in snowy weather, in North Eastern country. (*British Railways*)

One of the later 'Sandringham' class 4-6-0s with the larger tender, named after football clubs and allocated to the Great Central line: No 2862 *Manchester United*. (*British Railways*)

of the Holden 4-6-0s. The first batch of 'Sandringhams' was built by the North British Locomotive Co Ltd, so providing one of the very few instances of a new Gresley type being built other than at the railway company's own works.

At first the 'Sandringhams' did not have much opportunity for spectacular running. The night Continental expresses had by that time been decelerated, and other Great Eastern turns, strenuous enough for the Holden 4-6-0s, did not extend the 'B17s'. At the same time as high-speed trials were being carried out on the Great Northern main line, in preparation for the striking accelerations of May 1932, No 2800 made one or two fast trial runs on the Great Eastern section; apart from this, however, long mileages, and the same happy immunity from casualties as the Pacifics, characterised their early work. It was not until 1936, when the series named after leading Association football teams were turned out from Darlington works, that the 'B17s' took their true place in the records of British locomotive performances. This new batch was sent to Leicester shed, and the redoubtable enginemen who had made such a reputation for themselves with the ex-GCR. Atlantics took to the 'B17s' immediately, although, of course, they required quite different driving methods; their exploits on the 6.20 pm down from Marylebone have so shorn that train of its one-time difficulties from the locomotive point of view that before the war, loads of 400 tons went unpiloted. My own experiences on the footplate of several 'B17s' have shown their performance to be in the best Gresley tradition; no driver thought of working with anything but full regulator, and cut-off of 15 to 20 per cent produced the liveliest of running. Easily the most exciting trip I had was on No 2841 *Gayton Hall*, with the 2.32 am newspaper express. The details of this journey are given in the accompanying log, from which it will be seen that, with the exception of the climb over the Chilterns, in the amazing start out of Rugby and, of course, in the initial ascent from Marylebone to Brondesbury, the engine was worked on 15 per cent cut-off throughout. The running between Brackley and Rugby is a good sample of what such working produced, including such a *minimum* speed as 68½ mph at Charwelton. Then came that altogether extraordinary start out of Rugby, where the engine was given full regulator, and where 25 per cent cut-off was maintained to the top of the Shawell bank. By the LMS viaduct speed had risen to 51 mph, and a maximum of 66 mph was attained in 1¾ miles from the dead start, on a fall-

LNER 2.32 am Marylebone-Leicester

Engine: Class 'B17' 4-6-0 No 2841 *Gayton Hall*
Load: 271 tons tare, 300 tons full
Driver Simpson; Fireman Wood (Neasdon Shed)

Dist (miles)		Schedule (min)	Actual (min sec)	Speeds (mph)	Regulator	Cut-off (per cent)	Pressure (lb per sq in)	
							Boiler	Steam chest
0.0	MARYLEBONE	0	0 00	—	Full	65		
1.9	Canfield Place		4 30	33	Full	25	185	175
3.0	Brondesbury		6 10	32	Full	15		
5.1	Neasden Jc		8 32	70½	Full	15		
9.2	Harrow	13	12 34	53	Full	15		
11.4	Pinner		14 47	66	Full	15		
13.7	Northwood		17 00	59	Full	15		
16.2	Watford South Jc		19 11	75½	Shut	15		
17.2	RICKMANSWORTH		20 32	30	Full	30		
19.4	Chorley Wood		24 42	35	Full	30	185	175
23.6	Amersham		31 50	36	Full	15		
28.8	Great Missenden		36 51	77½	Full	15		
—	Dutchlands			63	Full	15		
33.3	Wendover		40 46	84	Shut	15		
38.0	AYLESBURY	44	44 13	—	⅓	15	185	100
44.1	Quainton Road Jc	52	49 26	56*	Full	15		
46.8	Grendon Jc		52 17	62	²/₅	15	180	120
				71	Full	15	185	175
54.5	Finmere		59 15	61½/73	Full	15		
59.3	BRACKLEY	67	64 45	—	—	—		
0.0			0 00		Full	65 to 25		
3.2	Helmdon		5 36	55		15	185	175
8.1	Culworth Jc		10 04	77		15		
9.8	WOODFORD & HINTON		11 27	72½		15		
12.2	Charwelton		13 32	68½	½	15		
19.2	Braunston		19 13	85	—	15	180	125
23.9	RUGBY	24	23 46	—	—	—		
0.0			0 00		Full	65 to 25	185	175
3.6	Shawell Box		4 47	66	Full	65 to 25		
6.8	Lutterworth		7 58	57½	Full	15		
15.2	Whetstone		14 45	90	²/₅‡	15	185	110
18.9	Leicester S Goods Jc		17 22	81	²/₅‡	15		
19.9	LEICESTER	20	19 02	—	—	—		

* Slight service slack   ‡ Regulator closed from full open to 2/5 near Ashby station

ing gradient of 1 in 176. After mounting the Shawell bank at a minimum of 57½ mph, the driver reverted to 15 per cent, and the run was fitly rounded off by a maximum of exactly 90 mph near Whetstone. In descending the final 1 in 176, full regulator was maintained for 2 miles from the summit, during which time we accelerated from 63 to 75 mph; then the regulator was partly closed, so that steam chest pressure dropped from 175 to 110 lb per sq in. With this latter pressure, in combination with 15 per cent cut-off, speed rose from 75 to 90 mph in 5 miles of 1 in 176 descent.

6

Experiments and rebuilds, 1927-33

While the broad principles of Gresley's standard practice were being developed, and duly embodied in new express passenger types, the quest for increased efficiency was being pursued in several other ways. To investigate the possibility of improving boiler performance, feed-water heaters of various types were tried; extended tests were made with poppet valves; and earlier experiments with boosters were followed by two particularly interesting applications. For a time, also, it seemed that Gresley was feeling his way towards some policy of boiler standardisation, since boilers of his own design were fitted to certain ex-GCR and ex-NER locomotives. The tests of feed-heating and poppet valves were made in a very practical way: their application to certain locomotive classes of moderate or indifferent performance improved the engines that were equipped from the operational point of view, and at the same time gave valuable running experience with the devices in question before any inclusion of them in first-line express passenger locomotives.

Before grouping, there was a Great Eastern 4-4-0 of the 'Claud Hamilton' class, No 1791, fitted with the Weir feedwater heater and pump, though this apparatus was removed in 1924. Isolated applications were also made of the Dabeg heater, on a Class 'O2' 2-8-0, and of the Worthington apparatus on an ex-Great Eastern 4-6-0, No 8509, and on an ex-North British Atlantic, No 9903 *Cock o' the North*. But the only type that was tried extensively was the ACFI. This was already in regular use on the Continent, and the observed performance of some 2,000 locomotives that were so fitted justified the manufacturer's claim that economies of 10 to 12 per cent in coal, and 15 per cent in water were realised, with the added advantage of a 10 per cent reduction in feed density when using hard water. These increases in efficiency were, of course, over similar locomotives on which the feed water was not heated at all. The LNER, however, was already using a form of feed-water heater in the Davies & Metcalfe exhaust steam injector which, while not giving so high an efficiency, was a great deal simpler. The tests were therefore to find out whether the higher service efficiency of the ACFI apparatus was enough to justify the higher initial cost.

Ex-NER Class 'Z' Atlantic No 2206, one of two fitted with the ACFI feed-water heater (*W.H. Whitworth*)

Two of the ex-NER three-cylinder Atlantics, Nos 728 and 2206 (Class 'C7'), were equipped, but Gresley's most extensive trials of the ACFI system were made on ex-GER 4-6-0 express engines of what is now LNER Class 'B12'. Whatever its effect in improving performance, the two cylindrical chambers saddling the boiler and the profusion of connecting pipes sadly impaired the handsome appearance of these engines, and was partly responsible for their being nicknamed 'Hikers', though this is sometimes claimed to be of Scottish origin. The drafting to the Great Eastern system of some 30 'Sandringhams' released a number of the 'B12s', and these were sent to Scotland for service on the GNS section. Here, limitation of axle loading had hitherto precluded the transference of more powerful types from other sections, and apart from the assistance of a few rebuilt Holmes 4-4-0s from the North British, the whole of the work in the far north-east was still being done by the little Manson and Pickersgill 4-4-0s. The Scottish enginemen found that on the 'B12s' coal had to be shifted quite

One of the Holden GER 4-6-0 locomotives fitted with the ACFI feed-water heater. (*Author's collection*)

a long way, in comparison, from the shovelling plate to the fire door; this distance, requiring a step or two on the fireman's part, is credited in Scotland with having given rise to the 'Hiker' nickname.

The results obtained were evidently encouraging, for Gresley carried the trials a stage further by equipping two of the Pacifics. From experience gained with the 'B12s' a number of modifications to the standard apparatus were suggested to the manufacturers, with the result that the two Pacifics were equipped with a considerably improved type of feed-water heater that was fitted inside the smokebox. This reduced the loss of heat due to radiation, to which the standard equipment, fixed in an exposed position on the boiler, was susceptible; the appearance of the engines was also much improved, as compared with the 'B12s'. These Pacific tests were of further value as giving results at two different boiler pressures, one engine, No 2576 *The White Knight*, being an 'A1' with 180 lb pressure, and the other, No 2580 *Shotover*, an 'A3', with 220 lb. This modified form of ACFI heater was also fitted to the first of the 2-8-2 express engines in 1934. Although no figures have been published, it would seem that any improvement realised in thermal efficiency over engines fitted with the standard arrangement of injectors was outweighed by the extra first cost and maintenance charges of the ACFI heater and its steam-driven pump; for since 1934 it has not been applied to any new engines. As in engine No 10000, and all Gresley's experimental work, once trials were embarked upon they were not lightly abandoned.

Concurrently, another series of tests was in progress on poppet valves, which on theoretical grounds could be arranged to provide a steam distribution nearer to the ideal than piston valves of the conventional type. The full valve opening, for example, was available no matter how early the cut-off, and more complete expansion of the steam was made possible by having the release position independent of the cut-off. The ex-GER 4-6-0s again featured in the first use of poppet valves on the LNER, No 8516

The LNER 'B12' 4-6-0 based on Holden's design, one of ten locomotives built in 1928 and fitted with Lentz OC poppet valve gear. (*Beyer Peacock & Co*)

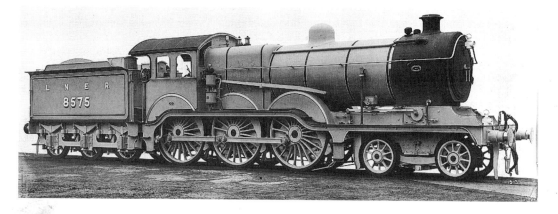

being equipped in 1927 with the Lentz oscillating-cam gear. As a result of this application, which gave valuable running experience, and a marked improvement in coal consumption, a batch of ten new 'B12s' having the Lentz OC valve gear was ordered from Beyer Peacock & Co Ltd. These engines, Nos 8571-8580, were put into service in 1928, and although in external appearance they conform generally to the original Holden design, the Gresley touch is apparent in the cutting away of the coupling-rod splashers. In the following year two of the ex-GCR four-cylinder 4-6-0s of the 'Lord Faringdon' class were fitted with the Caprotti valve gear, and this brought about a substantial improvement in the work of a class with a distinctly shaky reputation.

So far, it will be appreciated, the trial of poppet versus piston valves had not been made on equal terms, since the GC 4-6-0s, and the ex-GER 'B12s' could hardly be called modern engines. When turning out his own 'D49' class of three-cylinder 4-4-0s, Gresley equipped six of them with poppet valves driven by oscillating cams, the motion being provided by the usual arrangement of the Walschaerts gear. Direct comparison with the piston-valve engines was thus possible, and in 1929 the trials were carried further when two more 'D49s', No 336 *Buckinghamshire* and No 352 *Leicestershire*, were fitted with poppet valves operated by rotating cams. The driving mechanism for this gear was simple, consisting of a longitudinal shaft driven by a bevel gear off the driving axle, and it was probably on account of this simplicity that the RC gear received the most extended trial of all. As applied to 'D49' engines Nos 336 and 352, this gear provided only five positions of cut-off, ranging from 15 to 75 per cent in full gear, and it is not possible to work the engine with the gear between any two of these positions. In contrast to the Caprotti gear, which provides for infinitely fine adjustment anywhere between 3 per cent and full gear, the RC arrangement makes an engine somewhat inflexible in service. Yet the limitation so imposed in normal working cannot be unduly severe, for in 1932, when further 4-4-0 locomotives were required for intermediate service in the North Eastern Area, a new series of 'D49s' was turned out, all having the RC poppet valve gear. These engines were named after famous hunts,

'Hunt' class three-cylinder 4-4-0 No 336 as originally built with RC poppet valve gear and named *Buckinghamshire;* later renamed *The Quorn. (British Railways)*

Ex-GCR four-cylinder 4-6-0 No 1166 *Earl Haig* fitted by Gresley with Caprotti valve gear and renumbered No 6166 (*W.J. Reynolds*)

and their nameplates were distinguished by the figure of a fox above the lettering. The two experimental engines, Nos 336 and 352, were, at the same time, renamed *The Quorn* and *The Meynell* respectively.

On at least one occasion, however, the inflexibility of the RC poppet valve arrangement resulted in the failure of a locomotive to carry out a task of a special kind. About the time that the 'Hunts' were built, one of the ex-NER three-cylinder Atlantics, No 732, was rebuilt with a front end identical with that of the 4-4-0s, and one day in 1936 this engine was requisitioned for the up Silver Jubilee when the booked engine ran hot and had to come off at York. The driver found that one cut-off position was not sufficient to do the job, and the next, if used continuously, would 'just about have killed the fireman', to quote his own words. In this connection it may be recalled that in the only application of RC poppet valve gear made on the GWR, the two-cylinder 4-6-0 No 2935 *Caynham Court* had a mechanism giving nine instead of five cut-off positions, ranging from 10 to 85 per cent. The one-time

Class 'D49' three-cylinder 4-4-0 No 269 *The Cleveland* originally fitted with poppet valves driven through oscillating cams by Walschaerts motion. (*P. Ransome Wallis*)

Class 'D49' three-cylinder 4-4-0 No 359 *The Fitzwilliam* with RC poppet valve gear. (*P. Ransome Wallis*)

'uniflow' three-cylinder 4-4-2 No 2212 was also rebuilt with RC poppet valve gear.

Next to be recorded are the further experiments made with boosters. Great Northern Atlantic No 4419, the first LNER engine to have a booster, was fitted with one similar to those in fairly common use in America. This apparatus had a gear ratio of 2.57 to 1, and in extensive trials it was found that 15 mph was about the maximum speed at which the booster could be used; above that the demands on the locomotive boiler were too great owing to the high rotational speed of the auxiliary engine. That Gresley had in mind a method of operation differing considerably from that of contemporary American practice is clear from the specification he laid down for the booster equipment of some further Atlantic engines. An increased pull of 2 tons was to be provided on starting, and the booster had to be capable of cutting in smoothly at 30 mph, so that this speed could be sustained up a 1 in 96 gradient with a train-load of 400 tons. This envisaged the continued use of the ex-NER three-cylinder Atlantics of LNER Class 'C7' as reserve engines for the Anglo-Scottish expresses north of York, the booster to be brought into use on the Cock-

Ex-NER Raven Atlantic No 727 rebuilt by Gresley with a booster on the bogie, forming an articulation between engine and tender (and becoming Class 'C9'). (*British Railways*)

burnspath bank south of Dunbar, on the heavy grade just south of Durham, and, of course, in starting.

To do this the gear ratio of the auxiliary engine was, after considerable experiment and research, fixed at 1 to 1, on a machine having two cylinders 10½ in diameter by 14 in stroke. In 1931 two 'C7' Atlantics, Nos 727 and 2171, were equipped, a novel feature being that the booster engine was carried on a four-wheel bogie; the locomotive and tender were articulated with the rear end of the engine and the front end of the tender carried on this bogie. In rebuilding these two locomotives Gresley fitted enlarged boilers having 200 lb per sq in pressure, against the previous 170, and with grate area increased from 27 to 30 sq ft. Despite the reduction in the booster gear ratio the rebuilt 'C7s' had, with the booster in action, a higher nominal tractive effort than the 'C1' engine No 4419, owing to the greater cylinder volume and higher working pressure. On test one of the rebuilt 'C7s' started a load of 746 tons, exerting a drawbar pull of 12¼ tons, whereas with the booster cut out the drawbar pull in starting a load of 486 tons was 9 tons. Both these tests were made on level track.

A further development came in January 1932. For some time traffic conditions in the hump marshalling yard at Wath had been growing more arduous; here Robinson's ex-Great Central three-cylinder 0-8-4 tanks were at work, and the maximum load they could restart without assistance on the 1 in 107 gradient leading to the hump was 45 loaded 10-ton coal wagons. To handle increased loads in all weathers No 6171 of this class was rebuilt with a superheater-equipped boiler, and a reversible booster was fitted to the trailing bogie; all previous applications on the LNER for use in main line traffic had been of unidirectional boosters, though on an engine used for hump work it was obviously necessary that the auxiliary should be effective when working either chimney or bunker first. Another interesting feature of this rebuilding was that the bogie wheels were coupled, providing the auxiliary engine with valuable extra adhesion weight. With the booster in operation the nominal tractive effort of the locomotive was increased by 35 per cent, and its practical effect was to enable 62-wagon trains, about 1,000 tons loaded, to be operated successfully over the hump. Two new engines of the same type, Nos 2798 and 2799, were built at Gorton later in the same year; they were identical with No 6171, except that the side tanks were cut away at the front end to improve the driver's outlook.

Another interesting tank locomotive conversion, in 1931, was that of the ex-NER Class 'D' 4-4-4s, the first of which were built at Darlington in 1913. To assist in the handling of the heavy Teesside traffic these engines were altered to 4-6-2s, which change, while not adding to the nominal tractive effort, substantially increased the adhesion weight from 40 to 52¼ tons. Even before

LNER 0-8-4 tank locomotive No 2798, with reversible booster, used for hump shunting at Wath. (*British Railways*)

the conversion of the 4-4-4s there had been 4-6-2 tanks at work in this area. A batch of Class 'A5' engines was built specially by R. & W. Hawthorn Leslie & Co Ltd, showing once again Gresley's partiality towards Great Central designs; but in them the characteristically handsome Robinson outline was marred by the use of a 'Shire'-type built-up chimney, and a dome no higher than that of a Pacific.

Lastly, in connection with Gresley's modifications, certain changes in boilers require mention. In 1929 two of the ex-GCR 2-8-0s of Class '04', Nos 6287 and 6371, were turned out with Great Northern-type boilers, as used on the '02' engines. To accommodate these, the frames had to be lengthened at the trailing end, and in some further conversions a modified form of '02' boiler, with shorter barrel, was fitted. These later rebuilds retained their Great Central cabs, whereas Nos 6287 and 6371 acquired a curious-looking single-windowed affair. The rebuildings with modified '02' boilers proved successful, and since 1939 a considerable number of the class have been so altered; these conversions are classed '04/7'. A similar process was applied in 1929 to one of the Raven express passenger Pacific engines, No 2404 *City of Ripon*. This was not done in the interests of standardisation, for the North Eastern

Ex-NER Class 'D' 4-4-4 tank No 2162 rebuilt as a 4-6-2 and becoming Class 'A8'. (*British Railways*)

chassis was too long to allow of an 'A1' boiler being used. The new boiler was fitted to obtain better evaporation, by the use of a wide firebox and a barrel coned at the rear end. The advantages gained, however, were evidently not sufficiently marked to justify the continued existence of the 'A2s', and No 2404, in company with the four other engines, were scrapped some time ago.

The Royal Engine, No 8783, used for special trains between Kings Cross and Sandringham. (*W.J. Reynolds*)

7

New types, great and small, 1930-34

Towards the end of 1930 the first Gresley express tank locomotive was turned out from Doncaster works. Hitherto the company's needs in this category had been met by building more Class 'A5' 4-6-2s of the Great Central design; but although these engines, together with the converted Raven 4-4-4s, were holding the fort in the North Eastern Area, in Scotland there was certainly scope for something of more modern design than the Reid 4-4-2 tanks on the North British section, good engines though they were. Gresley followed Churchward's earlier example by building a tank engine version of one of his Mogul mixed-traffic types, and using the 2-6-2 wheel arrangement; though while producing an engine almost identical in tractive power to the 'K2s', Gresley adopted three-cylinder propulsion. The 'V1s', as they are classed, are compact and handsome engines with characteristically Great Northern lines. All three cylinders drive the middle pair of coupled wheels, and while the outside cylinders are inclined at 1 in 30 to the horizontal, the inside one is inclined at 1 in 8, so that the connecting rod clears the leading coupled axle. The three cylinders

Three-cylinder Class 'V1' 2-6-2 tank for Scottish area service: No 465. (*British Railways*)

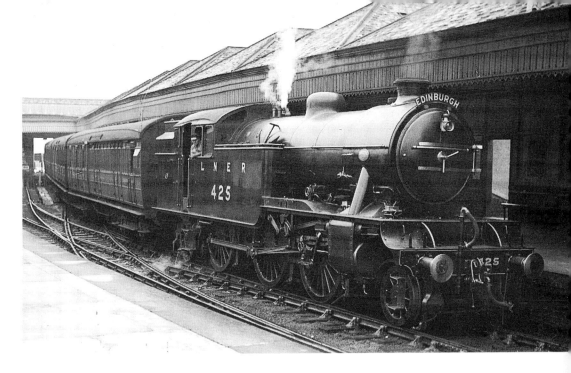

are combined in a single casting, a second steel casting forming the smokebox saddle and steam passages to the outside cylinders. The leading dimensions of the 'V1' engines are: cylinders (three) 16 in diameter by 26 in stroke; coupled wheels 5 ft 8 in diameter; valve travel, in full gear, $6^{1}/_{16}$ in; 22-element superheater, with a heating surface of 284 sq ft; total heating surface, 1,609 sq ft; grate area 22 sq ft; working pressure 180 lb per sq in. The side tanks have a capacity of 2,000 gallons, and the bunker carries 4½ tons of coal. In working order the total weight of the locomotive is 84 tons, of which 57 tons is available for adhesion. The nominal trac-

Class 'V1' 2-6-2 tank No 425 at North Berwick on a stopping train to Edinburgh. (*E.R. Wethersett*)

Class 'V1' 2-6-2 tank No 2909 at Dunbar. (*C.J.L. Romanes*)

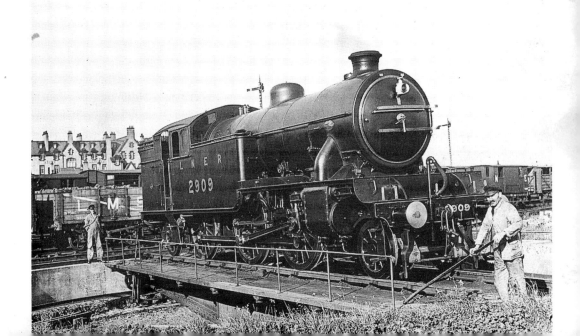

Class 'V1' 2-6-2 tank No 2916 on an up local train near Haymarket. (*C.L. Turner*)

tive effort at 85 per cent is 22,404 lb.

The performance of these engines was soon shown to be in the best Gresley tradition. Although the first batch was sent to Scotland, one of them, No 2911, spent a month at Kings Cross shed in the spring of 1931 and did some excellent work. Mr R.A.H. Weight timed her on a fast train up from Hitchin, when, among other smart performances, she passed milepost 7½, 10.2 miles from Hatfield, in 12 min 20 sec from the start. The load was 235 tons gross behind the engine, and after starting away uphill on 40 per cent, the cut-off was reduced to 15 per cent by Marshmoor; this, with full regulator, was enough to produce an uphill acceleration to 55 mph at Potters Bar summit. Later a maximum of 72 mph was reached below New Barnet. I myself have noted uphill and level running almost as good between Glasgow and Helensburgh, but lately the work of the 'V1s' has been eclipsed by that of the 'V3s', which are the same except that they have a working pressure of 200 lb per sq in.

In the London suburban areas of the GN and GE Sections, despite sporadic trials of ex-GCR 4-6-2 tanks working from Kings Cross, nothing larger than 0-6-2s were drafted until just before the war; the onus was shouldered almost entirely by the Gresley 'N2s', and the ex-GER 'N7s'. Building of the latter type continued long after the grouping. The accompanying table shows that the two classes were of markedly different design, and while both were used on the GN Section, the 'N7s' were especially suitable for the GE routes; they were well liked by the Running Department, so Gresley, with characteristic loyalty to his predecessors, whether Great Northern or of the other constituent companies, continued building these engines of A.J. Hill's design. There are now 134 of this class, of which the 32 built at Doncaster in 1927-8 have round-top fireboxes.

This reference to Great Eastern locomotives brings us to the important rebuilds of the 'Claud Hamilton' 4-4-0s and the '1500'

Comparative dimensions of 'N2' and 'N7' 0-6-2 tank engines

	'N2'	'N7'
Cylinders (in)	19 × 26	18 × 24
Coupled wheels (ft in)	5 8	4 10
Combined heating surface (sq ft)	1,205	1,072.3
Working pressure, (lb per sq in)	170	180
Grate area (sq ft)	19	17.7
Total weight (tons)	71½	64
Tractive effort (lb at 85 per cent BP)	19,945	20,512

class 4-6-0s, which were followed at a somewhat later date by the fitting of the ex-GER 0-6-0s of LNER Class 'J18' and 'J19' with boilers of Gresley design; the latter change was not accompanied by any reconstruction at the front end, however, save that the cylinder diameter was reduced from 20 to 19 in. All of Class 'J18' and all of 'J19' have now been rebuilt with Gresley boilers, and are classed 'J19/2'. As already related, the '1500s', now LNER Class 'B12', had been the subject of various trials, with poppet valves, and with feed-water heating apparatus. In view of this it is note-worthy that in the later and extensive reconstruction no special gadgets were fitted, but that the greatly improved performance was obtained by the use of a more efficient boiler and the re-design of the front end, at no greater increase in total weight than from 63 to 69¼ tons. The new boiler, with round-top instead of Bel-paire firebox, provides only a slight increase in total heating sur-face, from 1,834 to 1,874 sq ft, but the make-up of that inclusive figure has yielded a higher evaporation per lb of coal fired. The small flue tubes are enlarged from 1¾ to 2 in diameter; the grate area is increased from 26½ to 31 sq ft, and the increase in super-heating surface from 202 to 315 sq ft gives a higher steam temper-ature, with consequently greater fluidity and greater freedom in exhaust.

The new arrangement of the Stephenson link motion was arrived at after some preliminary experiments recalling the first trial of long-travel valves, on the 'A1' Pacifics. First, engine No 8559 was fitted with long-travel valves having a stroke, in full gear, of 6¹/₁₆ in instead of the original 4³/₁₆ in, the increase being obtained simply by making the arms of the rocking levers unequal. A con-siderably improved setting was subsequently obtained from a thorough re-designing of the gear, first fitted to engine No 8579 in 1932, in which the principal change was the use of expansion links having longer slots than previously. The table overleaf pre-pared from information kindly supplied by Mr E. Thompson, Chief Mechanical Engineer of the LNER, shows the valve setting of engines 8559 and 8579 in comparison with that of the original engines as built by the GER; one of the salient features, it will be seen, is that even when linked up to 15 per cent cut-off, the new valve setting provides an opening to exhaust equal to the full width of the port. The 10 in diameter piston-valves of the original engines have been reduced to 9½ in diameter in the new arrangement.

Valve gears on 'B12' 4-6-0 engines

Engine No	Total valve travel (in)	Width of ports (in)	Steam lap (in)	Exhaust lap (in)
8579	6.063	} 1¾	1.781	−0.098
8559	6.063		1.811	Line on line
8500	4.193		1.122	−0.187

Comparative records of valve readings

Approx Cut-off	Item	8579		8559		8500, etc	
		Front port	Back port	Front port	Back port	Front port	Back port
Full fore gear	Lead (in)	−.078	−.078	+0.16	−.047	+.141	+.078
	Max port opening to steam (in)	1.18	1.399	1.094	1.344	.883	1.062
	Cut-off (%)	72	69	68½	68½	72	71½
	Release (%)	93½	91¾	91½	90⅓	89½	88
	Max port opening to exhaust	Full	Full	Full	Full	Full	Full
	Compression starts (%)	90½	92½	90½	91½	93	94
	Total travel of valve (in)	6.078		6.062		4.195	
30% fore gear	Lead (in)	+.195	+.187	+.156	+.094	+.266	+.195
	Max port opening to steam (in)	.414	.453⅓	.391	.406	.344	.312
	Cut-off (%)	30	30½	28¼	32¼	28⅔	313
	Release (%)	77	743	76⅔	763	65	66
	Max port opening to exhaust (in)	Full	Full	Full	Full	1.625	1.656
	Compression starts (%)	72	74	76	76⅔	76½	76½
	Total travel of valve (in)	4.367		4.422		2.906	
15% fore gear	Lead (in)	+.234	+.227	+.203	+.125	+.281	+.219
	Max port opening to steam (in)	.289	.289	.266	.219	.281	.219
	Cut-off (%)	15	15	14½	15⅛	15⅛	15
	Release (%)	65½	63⅓	66	67¼	51½	52⅔
	Max port opening to exhaust (in)	Full	Full	Full	Full	1.531	1.594
	Compression starts (%)	60⅓	62½	67¼	66	66	64
	Total travel of valve (in)	4.078		4.110		2.75	

The valve arrangement fitted to No 8579 was tested carefully against that of No 8559 before a final decision was made. Coal trials made in August 1932 between Liverpool Street and Ipswich with trains of 385 tons tare showed an advantage of about 5 per cent in favour of No 8579; no dynamometer car was used, so that these figures, which were the coal actually consumed, could not be related to the drawbar horsepower developed. The trials were carried out on the 8.15 am down and the 12.23 pm up, both of which trains were then booked to make a number of intermediate stops; the 8.15 am took 110 minutes for the 68.7 miles, inclusive of five stops totalling 9 minutes, and 12.23 pm took 97 minutes inclusive of two stops totalling 6 minutes. In such circumstances the consumption by No 8579 of only 40.6 lb per train-mile on the round trip was good. In the same month No 8579 worked a load of 288 tons tare on the Yarmouth non-stop express, 12.30 pm ex-Liverpool Street, returning with the 4.30 pm up, non-stop from Beccles; on the round trip of 243½ miles, involving a running average of 47½ mph, the coal consumption worked out at the remarkable figure of 27.9 lb per train-mile. Considering the numerous hindrances to fast running on the East Suffolk line, this is a striking tribute to the efficiency of the new valve gear. The valve arrangement fitted to No 8579 was used for all engines subsequently rebuilt, and No 8559 was afterwards altered to correspond. The accompanying line diagram shows the general layout of the new gear in comparison with the old. In total effect the differences between the original 'B12s' and the rebuilds, which were classed 'B12/3', were so extensive that the latter may be considered as virtually new engines. Their handsome lines were set off by their being painted in passenger colours, and a pleasing reminder of their Great Eastern lineage remained in the polished brass beading over the splashers.

The 'B12/3s' are very fast and economical engines; but when

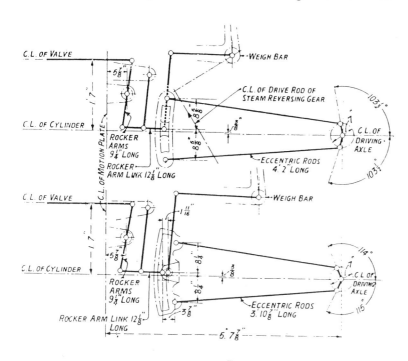

Figure 3 Diagram showing the general arrangement of the new valve gear on GER passenger locomotives as compared with the original.

Gresley's extensive rebuilt of a very famous Great Eastern locomotive, No 8900 *Claud Hamilton*, on an up Southend express near Chadwell Heath. (*E.R. Wethersett*)

comparison comes to be made with the original GER 4-6-0s it is no mean reputation that has to be surpassed. The nightly feats of the Parkeston drivers on the Hook Continental express will live in locomotive history, but there is no denying that the coal consumption was heavy, as a result of continuous working at 30 to 35 per cent cut-off. The 'B12/3s', like most Gresley engines, are worked on full regulator with 15 to 20 per cent cut-off; and as to speed, the first recorded attainment of 90 mph on Great Eastern metals stands to the credit of one of this class, No 8535, when a load of 305 tons was worked over the 46.3 miles from Ipswich to Norwich in a net time of 43½ minutes.

The renewal of certain engines of the 'Claud Hamilton' class, carried out, like that of the 'B12/3s', at Stratford works, was even more complete. Originally the former had slide-valves directly underneath the cylinders, whereas the new engines built on to the old chassis had new cylinders with piston-valves above, similarly to the 'B12/3s'. The first ten to be renewed, in 1933-4, including No 8900 *Claud Hamilton*, had 8 in diameter piston-valves with a maximum travel of 6^{1}/$_{16}$ in; but in a further ten, 9½ in diameter valves were fitted, in conjunction with re-designed cylinders having large steam and exhaust passages, and a degree of internal streamlining. No 8861 was the first of this later batch, and was turned out in April 1936. Both batches are now classed 'D16/3', though this classification also includes a number of rebuilt engines having the same enlarged boiler but retaining the original slide-

valves and power reversing gear. As with the 'B12/3s' the nominal tractive effort has not been increased above that of the original GER engines, but the improvement in performance, particularly that of the 9½ in valve batch, is very marked.

The November 1937 instalment of 'British Locomotive Practice and Performance' in *The Railway Magazine* includes a brilliant run by No 8808 of the latter variety, when, with a load of 280 tons, the 34.4 miles from Stowmarket to Norwich were covered in 34 min 37 sec start to stop, including a maximum speed of 84 mph; but, as with the 'B12s', the original engines were such grand runners that mere speed details provide no clue to the technical

Another rebuilt 'Claud', No 8860, on an excursion to Hunstanton near Great Chesterford. (*E.R. Wethersett*)

Class 'B12/3' 4-6-0, ex-GER, No 8516, rebuilt with the large Gresley boiler and improved front end. (*W.J. Reynolds*)

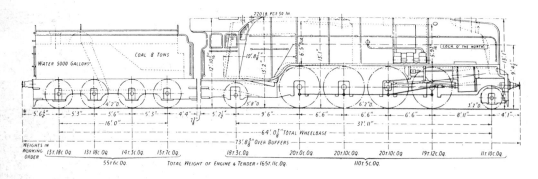

Figure 4 General arrangement diagram of No 2001 Class 'P2' as originally built.

The first Gresley 'P2' class express passenger 2-8-2, No 2001 *Cock o' the North*, built for service between Edinburgh and Aberdeen. (*British Railways*)

superiority of the new engines. In the same article of Mr Allen's are details of a run by No 8864, an unrebuilt superheater 'Claud Hamilton', in which Trowse, 45.3 miles from Ipswich, was passed in 42¾ min with a load of 245 tons, this including a maximum of 86 mph! A study of the cylinder design and motion arrangement of the 'D16/3s' with 9½ in valves leaves no doubt as to the potentialities of these new engines, and makes one speculate as to how they would do on the old Norfolk Coast Express timings, with the 400-ton loads worked by the 'Claud Hamiltons' in 1910-11.

In striking contrast to the trend of locomotive practice elsewhere, Gresley did not develop a policy of rigid standardisation of types. On the main lines, of course, his Pacifics, his 'K3' Moguls, and other types were already in widespread use, but where special conditions of road and traffic existed, he preferred to build special engines for the job, rather than use the largest standard type permissible, and double-head when required. Since the introduction of third class sleeping cars a serious operating problem had existed on the East Coast main line north of Edinburgh, where the heavy

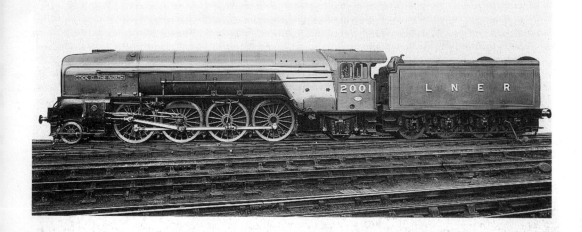

gradients compelled the limitation of Pacific loads to maximum tonnages of 440 tons southbound and 480 tons northbound.

The problem of designing a locomotive that would haul loads of 550 tons over that difficult road was not merely one of producing a machine big enough. The curves are as exacting as the gradients, and in any proposed design almost as much attention had to be given to its likely behaviour as a vehicle as to its haulage ability. The outcome of much careful research was the celebrated No 2001 *Cock o' the North*. This new locomotive was turned out of Doncaster works in May 1934 to a mighty fanfare of trumpets.

Cock o' the North running in on a local train from Kings Cross. An ex-GER design 'N7' 0-6-2 tank stands in the background. (*Author's collection*)

Cock o' the North preparing to leave Kings Cross on a down express. (*F.R. Hebron*)

Cock o' the North arriving at Kings Cross on an express from Leeds and Bradford. (*Author's collection*)

It was a time of intense effort by all the British railways to regain some of their lost traffic, when no chance of advertisement was to be lost. In the great size, unorthodox lines and challenging name of No 2001, the publicists found a plethora of material, and the engine duly featured in radio programmes and numerous high-coloured newspaper stories. The name was lifted from another Scottish engine, the North British Atlantic No 9903, which thereupon received the name of the pioneer of her class, *Aberdonian*, the latter having just been scrapped. *Cock o' the North* was the most powerful passenger engine in Britain at the time of construction, and that distinction is still held by the 'P2' class, of which No 2001 was the pioneer. Although broadly following established Gresley practice, the internal steam passages were streamlined to a greater extent than in previous LNER locomotives, and the freedom of the exhaust was increased by use of the Kylchap arrangement of double chimney and blastpipe. Equipment included the ACFI feed-water heater, and poppet valves operated by rotary cam gear, as in the 'Hunt' class 4-4-0s. The leading dimensions were: cylinders, (three) 21 in diameter by 26 in stroke; coupled wheels 6 ft 2 in diameter; total heating surface, 3,490 sq ft; grate area 50 sq ft; boiler pressure, 220 lb per sq in; total weight of engine and tender in working order, 165½ tons; tractive effort, at 85 per cent working pressure, 43,462 lb. In view of the soft exhaust which would result from the low back pressure aimed at, the smokebox was provided with an arrangement of aerodynamic screening to

lift the exhaust steam and smoke clear of the cab; *Cock o' the North* was not unlike No 10000 in this respect, though the latter engine had not the wedge-fronted cab that was later proved so efficacious as a smoke lifter on the 2-8-2s and the streamlined Pacifics.

The early days of the 'A1' Pacifics were soon vividly recalled by a heavy-load test run from Kings Cross to Grantham and back, with a 650-ton load. In the course of this trip a remarkable climb was made, from Peterborough to Stoke, with an average speed of 60.3 mph throughout from Tallington to the Summit box; during this fine exhibition a drawbar horsepower of no less than 2,090 was recorded. After this, service trials were conducted between Doncaster and Kings Cross, mostly on the up Yorkshire express then due at 1.55 pm, returning on the 4 pm down. On these trials *Cock o' the North* proved such a flyer as to astonish even those intimately connected with the design. Maxima up to 85 mph were attained with ease, a speed almost unheard of then with eight-coupled wheels. To the attainment of such speeds the poppet valves, with their exceptionally free exhaust, contributed largely, combining very effectively with the Kylchap double blast-pipes and chimney.

Cock o' the North went to Scotland in time to assist in the working of the August holiday traffic of 1934. At that time through locomotive working was in force between Edinburgh and Aberdeen, and a run on the up Aberdonian, timed by Mr W.A. Willox, showed the capabilities of the great engine to the full. With

Dynamometer test run with *Cock o' the North* on the 4 pm ex-Kings Cross at Peterborough. (*O.S. Nock*)

a load of 550 tons the 40.6 miles from Aberdeen to Montrose were covered in exactly 50 min start to stop, an average of 48.7 mph over that severe road that gave an arrival 8 min early at Montrose. The first sojourn in Scotland of No 2001 was short, however, for in December 1934 she was shipped across to France for trials at the Vitry testing plant of the OCEM. This step was in some ways to be expected, for not only was Gresley at pains to acknowledge his indebtedness to French practice for certain features of the design, but he was also one of the staunchest advocates of a similar testing station in this country.

8

The streamline era begins

In the autumn of 1934 the second 2-8-2 express engine, No 2002 *Earl Marischal*, was turned out from Doncaster works. It differed from *Cock o' the North* in several important respects. Instead of RC poppet valves, No 2002 had 9 in diameter piston-valves, with Walschaerts gear and the usual Gresley derived motion for the inside cylinder; and in place of the ACFI feed-water heater, No 2002 was fitted with a Davies & Metcalfe exhaust steam injector. Like No 2001, the second engine ran for some time between Kings Cross and Doncaster, and considerable trouble was experienced with smoke obscuring the driver's outlook. The aerodynamic screening at the front end, which had proved quite successful with the sharp exhaust from the poppet valves of *Cock o' the North*, was not so effective with the very soft blast of *Earl of Marischal*, which also had a double chimney and the Kylchap exhaust arrangement. A solution to the difficulty was found by adding side-plates somewhat similar to those used on the modern express locomotives of the Southern Railway. But the plates fitted to *Earl Marischal* proved to be a temporary measure only.

Before this there had been experiments with smoke-deflecting

The second 'P2' 2-8-2 No 2002 *Earl Marischal* at Ferryhill sheds, Aberdeen, with additional side shields. (*O.S. Nock*)

First attempts at exhaust steam deflection — 'A3' Pacific No 2751 *Humorist* with altered smokebox. (*British Railways*)

Humorist continued! No 2751 with double chimney and short wings, at Kings Cross. (*W.J. Reynolds*)

devices on the LNER. The serious accident to The Royal Scot at Leighton Buzzard in March 1931 drew attention to the trouble experienced on certain modern types of locomotive with smoke beating down, and although the standard Gresley Pacifics of the 'A1' and 'A3' classes did not generally suffer in this way, some experimental modifications were made to No 2747 *Coronach* and No 2751 *Humorist* in 1932. *Coronach* had the upper part of the smokebox cut away on a slope, after the style of the streamlined 'A4' Pacifics, though the original circular shell was retained to form a funnel, with the idea of inducing a strong upward current of air just behind the chimney. *Humorist* had a modified version of the same device, in which the smokebox shell was cut away and a trough, to produce the requisite air current, was made by fitting two inclined deflector plates to the smokebox top; this queer

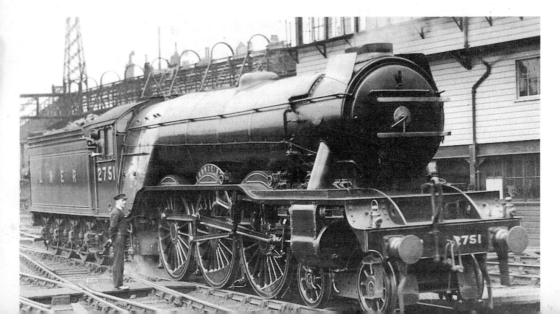

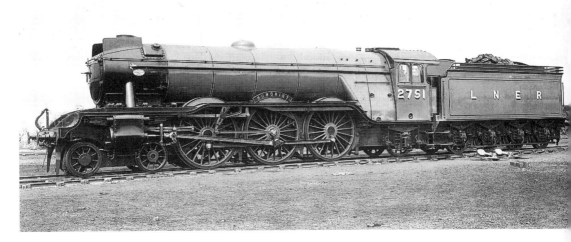

Above *Humorist* with single chimney and with the front of the smokebox tapered down, as modified in 1933. (*British Railways*)

Left Front view of *Humorist*. (*Real Photos Co Ltd*)

ensemble was completed by a perfectly plain stove-pipe chimney.

The normal smokebox was restored some years afterwards when *Humorist* was fitted with Kylchap double blast-pipe and an elongated version of the standard Pacific chimney; but the soft blast resulting from this exhaust arrangement compelled a return in 1938 to the small deflector plates, though this time with a normal round-topped smokebox. The absence of any lip on the elongated stove-pipe chimney was presumably to eliminate any projection that might cause eddies and so interfere with the lifting of the exhaust steam. From the footplate the effectiveness of the large deflector plates on *Earl Marischal* was obvious; the exhaust from the chimney was lifted by the inner screening, but at the same time given a lateral deflection, and the additional large plates provided an upward air current that counteracted the latter effect.

When No 2002 was handed over to the running department in Scotland in the early summer of 1935, she was a superb locomotive. On the 'A1' and 'A3' Pacifics there is usually a drop in pressure of about 10 lb per sq in between the boiler and the steam chests when the regulator is fully open; but on *Earl Marishcal* there was no drop at all—a striking tribute to the design of the steam passages. The riding, as I was able to observe on some footplate journeys, was easy and buoyant; indeed, it was more like that of a carriage than of a locomotive. As to the performance, there was the same sensitiveness to small changes in cut-off as is characteristic of the Pacifics. In this respect *Earl Marischal* showed up

Cock o' the North in regular service on the 2 pm ex-Edinburgh Waverley for Aberdeen, here seen near Inverkeithing. (*E.R. Wethersett*)

to be considerable advantage over the poppet-valve engine *Cock o' the North*; for, as with the RC poppet-valve gear fitted to the 'Hunt' class 4-4-0s, the 2-8-2 had a fixed cut-off corresponding to each cam, and no intermediate positions could be used.

Footplate observations on *Cock o' the North* showed that the driver worked at three positions, 18, 25, and 35 per cent, these changes of 7 and 10 per cent compared with the adjustments of 2 or 3 per cent at a time that produced such excellent results on *Earl Marischal*. It seems a pity that a gear capable of finer adjustment of cut-off was not fitted to *Cock o' the North*; for in the comparison the poppet-valve engine was certainly not operating on

LNER Aberdonian, Dundee-Edinburgh

Engine: 2-8-2 No 2001 *Cock o' the North*
Load: 493 tons tare, 530 tons full
Driver Shedden; Fireman Hardisty (Haymarket Shed)

Dist (miles)		Schedule (min)	Actual (min sec)	Speeds (mph)	Regulater opening	Cut-off (per cent)	Boiler pressure (lb per sq in)	Steam chest pressure (lb per sq in)
0.0	DUNDEE	0	0 00	—	3/5	65	190	180
0.8	Esplanade	—	3 02	19½	¾	25	200	200
	Top of 1 in 114	—	—		¾	18	—	—
2.7	*Tay Bridge S Junc*	8	7 38	33	¾	18	200	200
4.6	St Fort	—	10 32	61	3/5	18	195	180
8.3	LEUCHARS JUNC	14	14 22	55	Shut	—	—	Nil
		—	—	49	3/5	18	200	190
11.6	Dairsie	—	18 06	56	3/5	18	—	—
		—	—	60	Shut			Nil
14.6	Cupar*	—	21 10	55	3/5	18	195	180
16.9	Springfield	—	23 47	47½	3/5	18	—	—
		—	—	57	Shut	—	—	Nil
20.1	LADYBANK JUNC*	29	27 25	51	3/5	18	190	180
21.0	Kingskettle	—	28 21	60	3/5	18	—	—
23.1	Falkland Road	—	31 02	33	¾	18	195	190
24.3	*Lochmuir*	—	33 37	25½	Shut	—	—	Nil
25.9	Markinch Junc	—	36 02	52	Shut			Nil
	*Pitfall**	—	pws	12	Shut	—	—	Nil
28.5	THORNTON JUNC	41	40 42	—	¾	25	210	205
29.6	*Randolph Siding*	—	42 40	33	¾	18	—	—
31.2	Dysart	—	45 05	55	Shut	—	—	Nil
31.9	Sinclairtown	—	45 48	61	Shut	—	—	Nil
33.3	KIRKCALDY	—	47 07	65	Shut	—	—	Nil
34.4	*Invertiel Junc*	—	48 10	58½	Shut	—		Nil
36.5	Kinghorn*	—	50 27	25	Shut	—	—	Nil
		—	—	46	Shut	—	—	Nil
39.1	BURNTISLAND*	55	54 37	25	¾	35	205	200
		—	—	45	¾	18	—	—
41.8	Aberdour	—	58 59	33	¾	25	210	207
43.1	*Dalgetty Box*	—	61 29	31	Shut	18	—	Nil
		—	—	50	—	—	—	
46.2	Inverkeithing*	65	65 37	24	¾	25		
47.9	North Queensferry	—	69 52	19	¾	35	210	205
49.7	Dalmeny	73	73 24	42	¾	18	—	—
52.7	Turnhouse	—	76 40	68	¾	18	—	—
		—	—	59	¾	18	—	—
55.8	*Saughton Junc*	—	79 40	64	¾	18	160	150
58.0	Haymarket	82	81 47	—	Shut	—	—	Nil
59.2	EDINBURGH (Waverley)	85	84 57					

* Service slack

LNER Aberdeen-Dundee

Engine: 2-8-2 No 2002 *Earl Marischal*
Load: 479 tons tare, 515 tons full
Driver Arbuthnot; Fireman Conning (Dundee Shed)

Dist (miles)		Time (min sec)	Speed (mph)	Regulator opening	Cut-off (per cent)	Boiler pressure (lb per sq in)	Steam chest pressure (lb per sq in)
0.0	ABERDEEN	0 00	—	Full	65	190	190
0.6	Ferryhill Junc	2 19	—	Full	38	—	—
1.1	Milepost 240	3 28	30	Full	25	220	220
3.1	Milepost 238	6 55	37½	Full	25	—	—
4.8	Cove Bay	9 40	35½	Full	25	220	220
6.1	Milepost 235	11 48	38	Full	25	—	—
7.1	Milepost 234	13 18	41½	Full	20	215	215
8.2	Portlethen	14 33	—	¹/₅	18	215	170
10.4	Newtonhill	16 55	61	²/₅	18	215	160
11.6	Muchalls	18 05	61	¾	22	215	190
13.6	Milepost 227½	20 14	52	¹/₅	18	215	70
16.2	STONEHAVEN	23 24	†63	—	—	—	—
0.9	Milepost 224	2 46	28	Full	32*	195	195
1.9	Milepost 223	4 57	28½	Full	32	—	—
2.6	Dunnottar	6 16	32½	Full	25	220	220
2.9	Milepost 222	6 50	38	Full	25	—	—
3.9	Milepost 221	8 23	39	Full	25	—	—
4.7	Milepost 220¼	9 39	36	Full	25	215	215
5.5	Carmont	10 43	47½	⁵/₈	25	220	200
7.2	Drumlithie	12 50	—	¹/₅	18	220	80
11.2	Fordoun	16 43	64½	²/₅	22	190	150
14.5	Laurencekirk	19 59	60	⁵/₈	25	215 *	200
	Milepost 209¼	—	57½	¹/₅	18	—	80
17.7	Marykirk	23 11	64	—	—	—	—
19.8	Craigo	25 11	67	⁵/₈	20	190	180
21.9	Kinnaber Junc	27 50	15	—	—	—	—
24.5	MONTROSE	32 05	—	—	—	—	—
0.7	Milepost 30	2 03	26	Full	32*	215	215
1.7	Milepost 29	4 21	26½	Full	32	—	—
2.1	Usan	5 15	—	Full	27	—	—
2.7	Milepost 28	6 31	30½	Full	27	200	200
3.7	Milepost 27	8 26	32	Full	27	—	—
4.9	Lunan Bay	10 14	—	¹/₅	18	210	80
7.5	Inverkeilor	12 56	63½	½	22	200	175
10.7	Letham Grange	16 20	54½	¾	18	—	—
		—	62	¹/₅	18	200	80
13.1	St Vigeans Junc	19 00	20	¹/₅	18	—	—
13.7	ARBROATH	20 43	—	—	—	—	—

* 65 per cent for short distance from start   † Maximum before stop

equal terms with its piston-valve rival, and in these circumstances the subsequent conversion of No 2001 was practically inevitable. The accompanying tables give full details of two fine performances by the 'P2' engines in the summer of 1935.

The year 1935 was memorable in Gresley's career. It began with the brilliant performances of 'A3' Pacific No 2750 *Papyrus*, on the Kings Cross-Newcastle test runs in March; and midsummer saw the 2-8-2 express engines handling the heaviest loads with comparative ease on the Edinburgh-Aberdeen route. Yet few, if any, of the most ardent LNER enthusiasts were prepared for the events of late September 1935. The idea of a high-speed service between London and Newcastle was prompted by the striking success of

the high-speed diesel-electric railcars introduced in 1933 on the Union Pacific and Burlington Railroads in the USA, and on the German State Railway. Gresley was quick to realise the importance of these innovations, and personal experience of the running of the Flying Hamburger so impressed him that the question of purchasing a similar train for experimental purposes on the LNER was seriously considered.

In preparing, in the most detailed manner, a design for service in England, the makers of the German railcar were not able to promise a higher average speed than 63 mph between London and Newcastle, against the 77.4 mph of the Flying Hamburger between Berlin and Hamburg; the difference was due to the heavier gradients and speed restrictions of the LNER main line. Furthermore, the passenger accommodation was cramped, and hardly likely to attract passengers used to the spacious comfort of standard East Coast rolling-stock. In his Presidential address to the Institution of Mechanical Engineers in 1936, Gresley records how, at this stage in the investigation, Sir Ralph Wedgwood, then Chief General Manager of the LNER, suggested that with an ordinary Pacific engine faster overall speeds could be maintained with a train of much greater weight, capacity, and comfort. The *Papyrus* trial proved this contention to be correct, and that it might even have been possible to work a 4-hour service between Kings Cross and Newcastle by 'A3' engines, with a load of 200-220 tons.

At that time, however, the principle of streamlining, to reduce air resistance at high speed, was being applied to locomotives, and it seemed probable that some saving in power might be

Earl Marischal on the 10.20 am up East Coast express before leaving Aberdeen. (*O.S. Nock*)

effected by modifying the form of the standard Pacifics at the front end. Experiments were conducted at the National Physical Laboratory to determine a form that would both reduce air resistance and lift the exhaust steam effectively at high speed. The investigation, which was made with scale models, gave the following results, so far as air resistance was concerned:

Speed		60	70	80	90
Horsepower required to overcome head-on air resistance	'A3' 4-6-2	97.21	154.26	230.51	328.49
	Stream-lined 4-6-2	56.39	89.41	133.61	190.40
Horsepower saved by streamlining		40.82	64.85	96.90	138.09

These results indicated a probable saving in power output of about 10 per cent in the working of the new service, a forecast that was confirmed in practice. The now familiar wedge-shaped form has also proved most successful in smoke deflection; in this design an important feature is the slight depression immediately behind the chimney, without which it was found that, in a side wind, the eddy currents on the leeward side of the engine caused quite serious obscuring of the driver's outlook.

Furthermore, the publicity value of streamlining was an important point in attracting business to a new train service on which extra fares were to be charged for the privilege of higher speed. 'Streamline' was at that time a popular catchword, and its apparent sales value was reflected in the singular promiscuity with which it was applied, to toothbrushes, for example, domestic kettles, and even signalboxes! Into such a world emerged Gresley's new Pacific, No 2509 *Silver Link*. This apparition upset all one's well-established notions of what a locomotive, or at any rate a British locomotive, should look like; she provided a feast for the

Silver Fox, fourth of the original quartet of silver-painted 'A4' Pacific engines for the Silver Jubilee high-speed service. (*British Railways*)

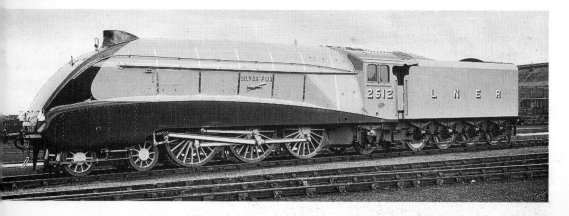

The down Silver Jubilee climbing the long bank to Potters Bar at the usual 65 mph and hauled by 'A4' 4-6-2 No 2510 *Quicksilver*. (*Rail Archive Stephenson, F.R. Hebron*)

sensation-mongers and a butt for the cynics who averred that the streamlining was merely a rather feeble pandering to popular taste. Among connoisseurs of the graceful in locomotive lines, many were genuinely appalled at this new development; and although the majority of railway enthusiasts have since become reconciled, their first reaction is still a vivid memory. In brief, the engine created a profound sensation.

The timing of the Silver Jubilee required speeds of 70 to 75 mph to be sustained up 1 in 200 banks, with a gross load of 235 tons behind the tender; on the level the schedule demanded sustained speeds of 85 to 90 mph. The locomotives would be working their hardest at 75 mph and over, in striking contrast to normal conditions on the heavy trains; and to provide for this some impor-

The two 10 am departures from Newcastle, abreast on the King Edward bridge in May 1936: on the left, 'A4' No 2512 *Silver Fox* on the Silver Jubilee, and on the right 'A1' No 2582 *Sir Hugo* on the London express that ran via Sunderland. (*W.B. Greenfield*)

Dynamometer car test run with the Silver Jubilee stock from Newcastle to Edinburgh on 26 September 1936, with engine No 2511 *Silver King* on Benton Bank. (*W.B. Greenfield*)

tant changes from the 'A3's were made in the design. The exhaust was made freer by the use of 9 in diameter piston-valves, against the previous 8 in, and the pressure drop between boiler and steam-chest was virtually eliminated by streamlined passages, as well as by the increased fluidity of the steam itself, due to the higher boiler pressure of 250 lb per sq in and a higher degree of superheat. The softer blast resulting from the freer exhaust would have created less draught in the firebox had the 'A3' boiler been retained, with, possibly, an adverse effect upon the steaming; so in the 'A4s' the boiler barrel was shortened from 19 ft to 18 ft, and the consequent reduction in tube heating surface was compensated for by the use of a combustion chamber. The cylinders of the 'A4s' were slightly smaller, of 18½ in diameter against 19 in.

In the haulage of the Silver Jubilee, the 'A4s' leapt into immediate fame. The trial run of 27 September, 1935 was only part of *Silver Link's* amazing début; then, although only three weeks out of the shops, she twice attained 112½ mph, and sustained an average of 100 mph for 43 miles on end.* A significant feature of the run was the average of 108.7 mph over the 10.6 miles from Biggleswade to St Neots, a stretch that includes as much adverse as favourable grading. Three days after this brilliant display she went into regular working on the Silver Jubilee, and duly performed the double journey, 536½ miles daily, for the first fortnight of the service. That this arduous duty was accomplished without any mechanical troubles was indeed a great tribute to design and workmanship. The Jubilee year, which had witnessed

*'The Silver Jubilee Express', *The Railway Magazine*, November 1935, page 353.

such a succession of triumphs for his locomotives, was fittingly crowned by the honour of knighthood conferred on Gresley himself, in recognition of his work, *The Times* happily expressing it 'as engineer and speeder-up to the LNER'.

Four streamlined Pacifics were built for the Silver Jubilee service, three of which were stationed at Kings Cross. The fourth, No 2511 *Silver King*, was spare engine and allocated to Gateshead shed; there she stood pilot for the up Jubilee, afterwards usually operating the long double-manned Newcastle-Edinburgh-York-Newcastle turn beginning with the 11.10 am non-stop express to Edinburgh. Although from the inception of the service it was clear that the 'A4' Pacifics were masters of their work, it was nearly a year later that the first technical details of their running were published. With the dynamometer car added to the train, increasing the tare load to 254 tons, trial runs were made between Newcastle and Kings Cross*, and Newcastle and Edinburgh. On the first run, on 27 August, 1936, No 2512 *Silver Fox* fractionally improved upon the maximum speed record of the previous September by attaining 113 mph in the descent of the Stoke bank. On the northbound trip on the same day No 2509 *Silver Link* made some outstanding running up the same incline; the 15.3 miles from Tallington to Stoke Summit were covered at an average speed of 82.7 mph with the locomotive working on 18 per cent cut-off and a wide open regulator. Both runs were made in ordinary service, and the speed of 113 mph attained by *Silver Fox* still remains the British record, by a considerable margin, for a train carrying fare-paying passengers. The work of No 2511 *Silver King* between Newcastle and Edinburgh included a most exceptional ascent of the Cockburnspath bank, in which 68 mph was sustained up the 1 in 96 gradient. This required a drawbar hp output of 1,460, whereas Gresley, in his Presidential address to the Institution of Mechanical Engineers, stated that the average dbhp required to work the Silver Jubilee between Kings Cross and Newcastle was no more than 620; in the Cockburnspath ascent, however, the pull of gravity on the locomotive and tender had to be overcome.

Until January 1937 there were only four engines of the 'A4' class, but in that month No 4482 *Golden Eagle* was turned out, the first of a new series, built for the Coronation express and general use on the fastest ordinary trains. Encouraged by the success of the Silver Jubilee, the LNER provided even more lavish passenger accommodation on the 6 hour London-Edinburgh flyer, bringing the tare weight up to 312 tons, against the previous 220 tons; this entailed considerably harder work, though it was coal

*'British Locomotive Practice and Performance', *The Railway Magazine*, December 1936, page 399.

One of the five new 'A4s' painted garter blue for the Coronation service, here seen hauling the up non-stop Flying Scotsman near Barkston, in August 1937: engine No 4492 *Dominion of New Zealand*. (*Rail Archive Stephenson, T.G. Hepburn*)

consumption rather than actual locomotive capacity that tended to govern performance on that train. It seems a little strange that on this hardest of all East Coast turns, the engines worked through from London to Edinburgh. With a normal consumption of about 3 lb of coal per dbhp-hr, roughly 7½ tons was burnt on that journey, and it did not need much in the way of cross winds or other adverse conditions to increase consumption to something very near the total capacity of the tenders—9 tons; indeed, on one occasion the up Coronation ran out of coal by Hitchin. Changing engines at Newcastle would have made all the difference. It was on the up Coronation that I recorded one of

The up Coronation near Low Fell with No 4489 *Dominion of Canada*, the bell ringing on the engine (*W.B. Greenfield*)

the most astonishing pieces of high-speed running that has ever been made with a British passenger train, under ordinary as against test conditions. That most famous of NE Area drivers, Walker, of Gateshead, was making his first trip on the train, and owing to over-emphasising some of the slacks we passed Grantham just over a minute late. With the engine working—so Walker told me afterwards—on 15 per cent cut-off, Stoke summit was breasted at 64½ mph; no change was subsequently made, and the engine accelerated superbly to 106 mph before Essendine. What made this descent so very exceptional, however, was the way in which the speed was sustained afterwards; for the aver-

Mr Vincent Massey, High Commissioner of Canada, with Gresley in the cab of *Dominion of Canada*. (*British Railways*)

Spectators admire No 4491 *Commonwealth of Australia* before departure of the up Coronation from Edinburgh Waverley. (*O.S. Nock*)

Right The up Junior Scotsman, the 10.05 am ex-Edinburgh, near Lamesley hauled by engine No 4464 *Bittern*. (*W.B. Greenfield*)

Below right The up Coronation entering Newcastle Central hauled by engine No 4498 *Sir Nigel Gresley* (*W.B. Greenfield*)

LNER 7.41 pm Grantham-York

Engine: Class 'A4' 4-6-2 No 4498 *Sir Nigel Gresley*
Load: 15 cars, 474 tons tare, 510 tons full
Driver Burfoot; Fireman Pearce (Kings Cross Shed)

Dist (miles)		Schedule (min)	Actual (min sec)		Speeds (mph)	Boiler pressure (lb/sq in)	Steam chest pressure (lb per sq in)	Cut-off (per cent)
0.0	GRANTHAM	0	0	00	—	215	215	65
2.3	Milepost 107¾	—	4	24	—	225	225	15
4.2	Barkston	—	6	31	62	—	—	—
6.0	Hougham	—	8	05	75	220	185	15
9.9	Claypole	—	11	08	82/74	—	—	—
14.6	NEWARK	15	14	47	79	shut off steam		—
			eased over troughs					
17.4	Bathley Lane	—	17	01	72	215	215	15
20.9	Carlton	—	19	46	77½	—	—	15
21.9	Crow Park	—	20	35	—	—	—	†20
26.4	Tuxford	—	24	39	62	—	—	25
28.2	Markham	—	26	22	64	225	225	15
30.0	Gamsten	—	28	00	—	225	225	15
32.0	Grove Road	—		—	82	shut off steam		—
33.1	RETFORD	32½	30	44	*47	220	220	25
34.1	Canal	—		—	—	220	220	15
36.2	Sutton	—	34	17	64	—	—	15
38.4	Ranskill	—	36	18	66½	—	—	15
40.3	Scrooby	—	37	52	75	210	210	15
42.2	Bawtry	—	39	27	69	210	210	20
44.0	Milepost 149½	—	41	04	67	—	—	15
45.8	Rossington	—	42	37	77½	—	—	15
47.7	Black Carr Junc	—	44	07	—	—	—	—
50.5 / 0.0	DONCASTER	50 / 0	48 / 0	47 / 00	—	— / 235	— / 235	— / 60
2.1	Arksey	—	4	28	—	235	235	18
4.2	Shaftholme Junc	—	6	46	62½	—	—	15
7.0	Moss	—	9	22	69½	—	—	—
10.0	Balne	—	11	53	75	230	230	—
11.3	Heck	—	12	56	71½	—	—	—
13.8	Templehurst	—	15	01	74½	235	235	—
17.0	Brayton Junc	—	17	36	‡79	—	—	—
			sigs		20	—	—	—
18.4	SELBY	20	20	10	—	235	235	35
19.1	Barlby Junc	—	21	26	—	—	—	15
25.1	Escrick	—	27	53	66	230	230	—
28.0	Naburn	—	30	25	70½	—	—	—
30.2	Chaloners Whin Junc	—	32	26	—	—	—	—
			sigs		—	—	—	—
32.2	YORK	37	36	43	—	—	—	—

* Service slack   † Advanced to 20 per cent 2 miles *beyond* Crow Park station   ‡ Before Brayton Jc

age speed from Essendine to Helpston Box was no less than 104.8 mph. About half this distance of 6.7 miles is downhill at 1 in 264 and 1 in 440, but between Tallington and Helpston, where we continued running at 105-106 mph, the gradient changes between 1 in 528 and dead level. The engine was No 4491 *Commonwealth of Australia*, and the gross load 325 tons.

As an example of the work of the 'A4s' in ordinary East Coast service, I have tabulated above very full details of a footplate journey on No 4498 *Sir Nigel Gresley* on the 5.45 pm from Kings Cross. On this occasion a maximum of 79 mph was attained on level track with the engine working on 15 per cent cut-off. This per-

Mallard with the dynamometer car test train at Barkston, ready for the 126 mph record run. (*Westinghouse Brake & Signal Co*)

The men who made the record: left to right, Fireman Bray, Driver Duddington, Locomotive Inspector Jenkins. (*Westinghouse Brake & Signal Co*)

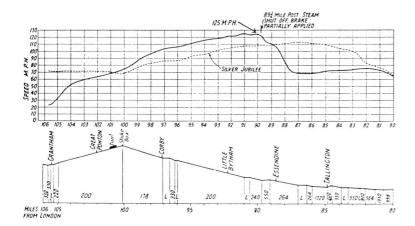

Figure 5 Speed curves of *Mallard* (240 tons), 3 July 1938, compared with *Silver Link* (270 tons), 27 August 1936.

formance, involving an output of 1,760 dhp, was an impressive exposition of the capabilities of these engines.

Four engines of the class were fitted with double chimneys and the Kylchap exhaust arrangements, and several of the finest performances yet recorded with Gresley Pacifics have been made by members of this quartet. No 4468 *Mallard* on 3 July, 1938, secured for Britain the world's record speed with steam by attaining 126 mph on a test run down Stoke bank. No 4901 *Capercaillie*, working a colossal wartime load of 665 tons tare and 730 tons gross, averaged 75.9 mph over the 25 miles from Otterington to Poppleton Junction; this achievement over an almost level road must have involved a continuous output of about 2,100 dbhp. On a footplate journey with No 4902 *Seagull*, on the 1.20 pm down Scotsman, we were running past Hitchin on 16 per cent cut off, with the regulator partly closed, and yet were accelerating at such a rate as to increase the speed from 84 to 95 mph in three miles; indeed, with the controls unchanged it is possible that we might have gone over the hundred at Arlesey, 480-ton load notwithstanding, had not the driver almost closed his regulator just below Cadwell in order to keep to the 90 mph limit.

9

The 'big engine' policy continued

The form of the streamlining used at the front end of the 'A4' Pacifics proved so successful in deflecting the exhaust steam clear of the cab that it was applied to four further 2-8-2 express locomotives, built in 1936. These engines were otherwise similar to No 2002 *Earl Marischal*, and bore equally fine Scottish names: *Lord President, Mons Meg, Thane of Fife* and *Wolf of Badenoch*. The last mentioned, No 2006, was fitted with a boiler having a longer combustion chamber than that of the other five engines. As had been expected, the front-end streamlining proved as effective as on the 'A4s', and Nos 2001 and 2002 were subsequently modified to conform with the rest of the class; at the same time No 2001 *Cock o' the North* had the valve motion changed from the RC poppet gear to Walschaerts, with the usual Gresley derived motion for the valves of the inside cylinder. The later 'P2' engines anticipated, to a certain extent, the latest modification to the 'A4s', wherein the valance over the driving wheels has been removed. In the 'A4s', however, the shrouding has been cut away also between the cylinders and the buffer beam.

With six Mikados available, the motive power problem on the

The first of the later batch of 'P2' 2-8-2s, No 2003 *Lord President*, showing the handsome streamlined front end. (*British Railways*)

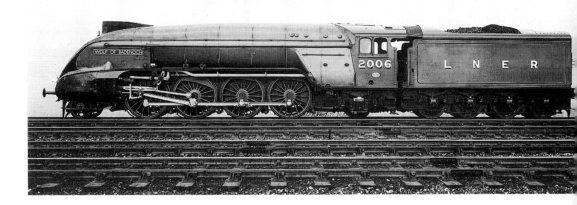

Edinburgh-Aberdeen route was greatly eased, and several very heavy turns, hitherto entrusted to Pacifics, henceforth became 'P2'-hauled. At the same time, due to return workings, they were not always employed on exceptionally heavy trains, as had been the case when *Cock o' the North* and *Earl Marischal* were holding the fort alone. The 9 am from Aberdeen was often hauled by a 'P2' between Dundee and Edinburgh and, with its winter load of little more than 200 tons, provided the easiest of jobs; indeed, on one occasion when the load was 215 tons, Mr Cecil J. Allen timed No 2004 *Mons Meg* at a sustained 53 mph up the 1 in 100 gradient past Aberdour to Dalgetty summit, where speed is normally about 30 mph. The 'P2s' are rostered to haul loads up to 550 tons tare in each direction between Edinburgh and Dundee, although, in the up direction, a bank engine must be provided up to the Forth Bridge, if for any reason one of these heavy trains has to stop at

Class 'P2' 2-8-2 No 2006 *Wolf of Badenoch* with the enlarged combustion chamber. (*British Railways*)

Cock o' the North, after modification of the front end, crossing the Royal Border Bridge at Berwick *en route* from Doncaster Plant Works to Edinburgh. (*E.R. Wethersett*)

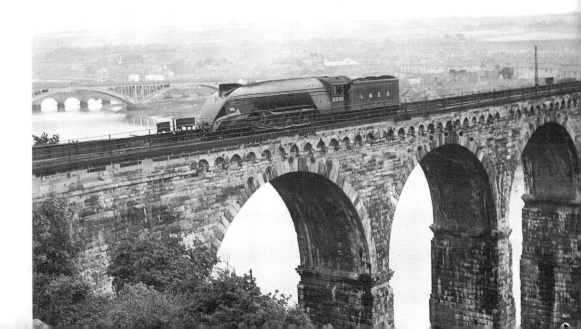

Class 'P2' 2-8-2 No 2003 *Lord President* on the 10.25 am Aberdeen-Edinburgh express near Laurencekirk. (*M.W. Earley*)

Inverkeithing. Between Dundee and Aberdeen the maximum rostered load is slightly reduced, to 530 tons in each direction.

At about the same time as No 2003 *Lord President* was turned out, there appeared the first of the 2-6-2 express engines, No 4771 *Green Arrow*. As was the case with nearly all Gresley's most successful designs, very few of these locomotives were built until thorough service trials had been carried out. Of the 'Green Arrows', Class 'V2', only five were built in 1936. These were stationed at widely-separated depots, and fore-shadowed the eventual use of the new class as express passenger and mixed traffic engines over the entire East Coast route. No 4771 was stationed at Kings Cross, 4772 and 4773 at York, 4774 at Peterborough, and 4775 at Dundee. Although they are designated mixed-traffic engines, the use of 6 ft 2 in coupled wheels, in combination with an efficient modern front end, makes them eminently suitable for any express passenger duty, except perhaps the streamlined trains. The design is derived, to a large extent, from that of the 'A3' Pacifics, although some interesting variations are shown by the following table:

Comparative dimensions of 'V2' and 'A3' class locomotives

	'V2' Class 2-6-2	'A3' Class 4-6-2
Cylinders (three) (in)	18½ × 26	19 × 26
Coupled-wheels, diameter (ft in)	6 × 2	6 × 8
Total wheelbase (engine) (ft in)	33 × 8	35 × 9
Total length over buffers (engine and tender) (ft in)	66 × 5	70 × 5
Length of boiler barrel (ft)	17	19
Total evaporative heating surface (sq ft)	2431	2736.6
Grate area (sq ft)	41¼	41¼
Boiler pressure (lb per sq in)	220	220
Adhesion weight (tons cwt)	65 × 12	66 × 3
Weight of engine in working order (tons cwt)	93 × 2	96 × 5
Weight of engine and tender in working order (tons cwt)	144 × 2	154 × 3
Nominal tractive effort at 85 per cent working pressure (lb)	33,730	32,909

A study of these dimensions reveals once again Gresley's then well-established practice of working out each new design entirely on its merits, without any particular concern for the possible incorporation of existing standard parts. By making the cylinders of the 'V2s' ½ in larger in diameter, the front end could have been made interchangeable with that of the 'A3s'; but in that case the cylinder volume would have been disproportionately large in relation to the evaporative heating surface, which, with a boiler barrel shorter by 2 ft, was less than that of the 'A3s' by 305 sq ft. So an entirely new front end design was prepared, in which the cylinders, steam-chests, smokebox saddle and outside steam-pipes were incorporated in a single steel casing. The boiler is of the same diameter as that of the 'A3' class; the shortening takes place in the parallel portion at the front end. As in the 'P2s', and in the final batch of 'A3s', the boiler is fitted with a steam collector instead of a dome, and through this collector must pass all steam entering the regulator. This device has proved very effective in counteracting any tendency to prime, and, to minimise any wire-drawing effects at the point of entry to the collector, the cross-sectional area of the slotted holes cut in the top of the boiler barrel-plate is double that of the full regulator opening.

It will be seen that, although the 2-6-2 wheel arrangement was used, the total engine wheelbase is only 25 in less than that of the Pacifics. This is partly accounted for by the spacing of the coupled wheels; in the 'A3s' the driving axle is 7 ft 3 in from both the leading and trailing coupled axles, whereas in the 'V2s' the

The first 'V2' 2-6-0, No 4771 *Green Arrow*, on the afternoon Scotch Goods, at Hitchin, awaiting the passing of the Coronation. (*O.S. Nock*)

trailing coupled axle is 8 ft 3 in from the driving axle. In comparison with the original 'A3s' their appearance suffers somewhat from the height of the running plate, which leaves the coupled wheels completely exposed, and from the shape and position of the steam collector; a touch of distinction is provided, however, by the wedge-shaped front of the cab, so designed to induce air currents for deflecting any exhaust steam which tends to beat down. Taken all round, the 'Green Arrows' embody, in a single outstanding design, every feature that Gresley, in his long career, had found to give efficient and reliable service. The only possible omission was the Kylchap double blast-pipe and chimney, although, at the time *Green Arrow* was built, that device was still only in experimental use on the LNER.

In regular express passenger service before the war their work was practically indistinguishable from that of the Pacifics. At first they were chiefly to be seen on relief portions of regular trains, but their running in these circumstances was such that, as more became available, they were regularly drafted to top-link duties; the Yorkshire Pullman, with its 60 mph timing between Doncaster and Kings Cross, was a case in point. With loads of about 400 tons, their speeds down the Stoke bank were just as fast as those of the Pacifics on the Leeds Breakfast Flyer. Details were published in *The Railway Magazine* of a run by No 4817 on which a maximum of 93 mph was attained near Essendine, and the 17.6 miles from Corby to Werrington Junction were run at an average speed of 86.2 mph. The load behind the tender on this occasion was 380 tons gross. Speeds of 90 mph were not uncommon with 'V2s' on the Great Central section also. With the exception of the special test runs with engines Nos 4472 and 2750 before the introduction of the Silver Jubilee service, speeds of 90-92 mph also seem to be about the maximum regularly attained by the 'A1' and 'A3' Pacifics, and thus it would appear that air resistance, rather than piston speed, is the limiting factor, where other considerations, such as front-end design, are equally favourable. A piston speed equivalent to that of No 4817 at Essendine would be equal, with a Pacific, to 101 mph.

It is significant of the versatility of the 'V2s' that their work on first-class express passenger traffic has come so much into the limelight. In connection with express goods traffic, I was fortunate in having an opportunity of observing the work, between Kings Cross and Peterborough, of *Green Arrow* herself, on the famous 3.35 pm down Scottish goods. The running made on that occasion has a special significance today, for the similarity of the load to those of wartime East Coast expresses helps to show how easily the 'V2s' can make the moderate speeds now demanded. I should add, however, that on my 1937 trip *Green Arrow* was in the 'pink' of condition. From Sandy to Peterborough we had a load of 47 vehicles, all four-wheelers; the actual gross load was estimated at 610 tones, but, having due consideration for the higher frictional resistance of goods wagons, this would have been equal to about 700 tons of bogie passenger stock. With this load *Green Arrow* ran at 62 mph on the level, on 18 per cent cut-off, with the regulator only partly open, and with 160 lb per sq in in the steam-chest as against a boiler pressure of 220 lb per sq in. The acceleration out of Sandy also was most impressive. The engine was started on 65 per cent cut-off, with the regulator opened to give 140 lb per sq in in the steam-chest. After about 200 yards the regulator was opened to the full, linking-up began, and, exactly a mile out, the cut-off was down to 18 per cent. This adjustment was maintained as far as Tempsford, 3.4 miles, where the regulator was partly closed; by that time the speed was 53 mph. In the earlier stages of the journey, with a lighter load of 42 vehicles, 550 tons behind the tender, the hill climbing also had been very good; details of the working again show complete mastery over the load. The start from Kings Cross Goods Station was made on 65 per cent cut-off, and a partly opened regulator, but, as soon as the train was on the move, and, indeed, before we entered Copenhagen tunnel, the cut-off was shortened to 40 per cent and the regulator opened to the full. As we gathered speed, the cut-off was reduced by steps of 2 or 3 per cent until it was down to 25 per cent on passing Holloway summit; yet, notwithstanding this comparatively easy steaming, we averaged 18 mph up the 1 in

Engines for the Coronation and the Scotch Goods abreast at Kings Cross Top Shed: 'A4' No 4490 *Empire of India* and 'V2' No 4771 *Green Arrow*. (O.S. Nock)

107 gradient between Belle Isle and Holloway North Down box. Belle Isle, of course, was passed at no more than a walking pace, as we had started from the goods terminus. Full details of the running are given in the following log.

LNER 3.35 pm Kings Cross (Goods)-Peterborough

Engine: Class 'V2' 2-6-2 No 4771 *Green Arrow*
Load: to Sandy 42 vehicles, 550 tons gross; to Peterborough 47 vehicles, 610 tons gross
Driver Hart; Fireman Cook (Kings Cross Shed)

Dist (miles)		Schedule (min)	Actual (min sec)	Speeds (mph)	Cut-off (per cent)	Regulator	Pressure (lb per sq in)	
							Boiler	Steam chest
0.0	KINGS CROSS (Goods)	0	0 00 Sigs	—	65	Full	175	170
2.0	Finsbury Park	—	6 43 Sigs	—	18	—	—	—
4.4	Wood Green	—	11 06	45½	18	—	195	190
8.6	New Barnet	—	18 48	35¼	18	—	—	—
12.1	Potters Bar	—	24 12	32	18	½	190	120
17.1	HATFIELD	30	30 18	63	18	Full	195	185
22.9	Woolmer Green	—	37 04	20*	18	—	—	—
30.6	Hitchin South	53½	58 50	—	—	—	—	—
0.7	HITCHIN	4	3 00	—	18‡	³/₅	200	140
4.5	Three Counties	—	9 46	57/53	18‡	²/₅	195	100
9.9	Biggleswade	—	15 40	62	18‡	²/₅	195	100
12.9	SANDY	35	19 35	—	—	—	—	—
3.4	Tempsford	—	6 18	53	18	Full	200	195
7.6	St Neots	18½	11 12	48¾	18	½	200	130
11.9	Offord	—	15 56	59	18	⁷/₈	—	—
14.8	HUNTINGDON	30	18 56	—	18	—	200	185
17.9	Post 62	—	22 54	46	18	—	—	—
19.4	Abbotts Ripton	—	24 39	—	18	¼	200	75
25.3	Holme	—	30 34	66	18	³/₅	185	160
28.5	Yaxley	—	33 53	—	18	—	185	160
32.3	PETERBOROUGH	—	38 40 Sigs	—	18	—	185	160
33.0	Westwood Jc	54	42 00					

* Crossover slack to slow line   ‡ Linked up to 18 per cent near Cadwell Box

This performance makes an interesting comparison with that of an 'A1' Pacific with a 520-ton load. The latter engine, on the 1.20 pm Scotsman, passed Belle Isle in full cry, with wide open regulator and 47 per cent cut-off; by Holloway summit her driver had linked-up to 28 per cent, yet, even with this flying start, his average over the same section was only 21½ mph. The steam-chest pressures recorded on *Green Arrow* were indeed a tribute to the design of the steam passages, for with full regulator there was never a drop of more than 5 lb per sq in between the boiler and the steam-chest.

In explanation of our apparently wholesale disregard of schedule time north of Hitchin, allowance is made for sidetracking, if necessary, to clear the way for the Yorkshire Pullman. In addition to being delayed somewhat on the slow line between Woolmer Green and Hitchin South, we were held longer than usual owing to the 4 pm down Yorkshire express being divided. On this account we were only just on time at Sandy. From there onwards, however, Driver Hart certainly showed off the paces of his engine, and incidentally showed the Yorkshire Pullman a very clean pair of heels.

On the Edinburgh-Aberdeen route the 'V2s' were rostered to take the same loads as the 'A1' and the 'A3' Pacifics. The maximum tonnages are of interest when compared with those laid down for other classes over this route, as shown in the following table:

Maximum tonnages allowed over the Edinburgh-Aberdeen route

	'D49' Class 4-4-0	'C11' Class 4-4-2	'A1' and 'A3' Class 4-6-2	'V2' Class 2-6-2	'P2' Class 2-8-2
Aberdeen to Dundee	310	340	420	420	530
Dundee to Edinburgh	340	370	450	450	550
Edinburgh to Dundee	340	370	480	480	550
Dundee to Aberdeen	340	370	480	480	530

Limits are also laid down for the 'D49' class when piloted. Two 'D49s' are allowed to work in double-harness north, but not south, of Dundee; the maximum tonnage for such a pair is 600 northbound, and 550 southbound. The same limits apply south of Dundee for a 'D49' piloted by a 'B12' ex-GER 4-6-0. Now that the North British Atlantics of Class 'C11' have been scrapped, nothing larger than a 'D49' may be piloted. Due to their shorter wheelbase and general handiness, the 'V2s' have become very popular on this route, and they work passenger and express fish and other fast freight trains turn and turn about with the Pacifics. These duties are tyical of their widespread use over the LNER system.

On the Great Central section, the Leicester top-link enginemen, as might be expected, have made some very fast runs with 'V2s' on the pre-war 6.20 pm down express from Marylebone, and have worked them up to 90 mph as readily as the Great Northern men

On the GW & GC Joint line: a 'V2', No 4830, on the 6.20 pm Marylebone to Bradford express approaching Saunderton. (*H.K. Harman*)

seem to do. But perhaps the most outstanding performance yet in high-speed passenger service took place when No 4789 was drafted at very short notice to work the streamlined West Riding Limited on its 68½ mph start-to-stop booking from Kings Cross to Leeds. A number of delays were experienced *en route*, but the net time was estimated at 167 min for the 185.7 miles, within 4 min of booked time and involving an average speed from start to stop of 66.7 mph . The load was the usual one of 278 tons tare, 290 tons gross. Shortly before the outbreak of war a similar case occurred in the North Eastern area, when another 'V2', No 4782, worked the down Coronation forward from York. Under present traffic conditions the 'V2s' are interchangeable with the Pacifics on all the heaviest duties, and through Gresley's 'big engine' policy the LNER, with over 130 'V2s' now in service, is fortunate in having nearly 250 locomotives capable of handling the entire present range of main line duties, that is to say on routes where engines of such weight can be operated.

At the close of 1937 Gresley carried his policy still further with the reconstruction of engine No 10000 as a three-cylinder simple. Little except the chassis of the original engine was retained. The new boiler was very much, although not exactly, similar to those of the 'P2s', having a total heating surface of 3,346, against 3,490 sq ft; the grate area was 50 sq ft in both classes. The new cylinders were 20 in diameter, as in the 'A1' Pacifics, and this, in combination with a boiler pressure of 250 lb per sq in, made the rebuilt No 10000 the most powerful high-speed locomotive in the country, as the nominal tractive effort, at 85 per cent of working pressure, was 41,437 lb. Its potentialities were further increased by the use of the Kylchap double blast-pipe and chimney, although with such large cylinders it is a little surprising that the piston

The 'hush-hush' 4-6-4 completely rebuilt in 1937 in garter blue, then Class 'W1'. (*W.J. Reynolds*)

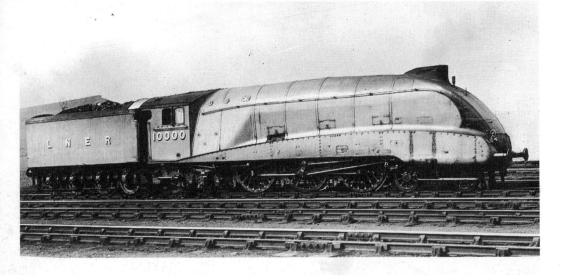

valves were made only 8 in diameter as in the 'A1s' and 'A3s' whereas the 'A4s', with 18½ in diameter cylinders, had 9 in valves. Up to the present time no recorded performance of No 10000 has equalled, let alone eclipsed, the maximum efforts of the 'A4s', and I cannot help feeling that the size of the valves might prove a bottleneck in the steam-flow circuit which would prevent the development of a power output commensurate with the nominal tractive effort and the proportions of the boiler and firebox. One has in mind performances such as that of Kylchap 'A4' No 4901 *Capercaillie* referred to previously. Providing the boiler can produce the necessary steam, the 4-6-4 engine should be able to haul a greater load in proportion to her increased tractive effort, and at the same speed; so that, on the basis of *Capercaillie*'s performance— an average of 75.9 mph over the 25 miles from Otterington to Poppleton Junction, with 730 tons—No 10000 ought to be able to make the same speed with 850 tons.

Loads of this magnitude are approaching transatlantic standards, and one thinks immediately of the Pennsylvania 'K4' Pacifics, which are limited to a maximum load of 870 tons. But, assuming it were possible for No 10000 with her present front-end arrangements to develop continuously the horsepower needed to work an 850-ton load at such speeds, the coal consumption would probably be beyond the range of hand-firing. Station facilities rather than locomotive capacity are likely, however, to prevent express train loads from rising much above 550-600 tons in normal times, and the great power of No 10000 has found, and will continue to find, its most useful application in accelerating heavy trains from rest, and in the making of exceptional uphill efforts.

A very strking example of this attribute was recorded by Profes-

An 'A1' on the Coronation in June 1938, No 2575 *Galopin* near Low Fell. (*W.B. Greenfield*)

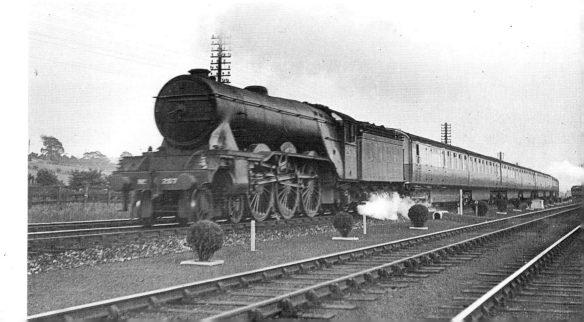

An 'A3' on the Silver Jubilee — No 2501 *Colombo* passing Peterborough on time with the up streamliner. (*Rail Archive Stephenson, T.G. Hepburn*)

sor E. S. Waterhouse on the wartime 9.50 am down Scottish express from Kings Cross. With a 20-coach train of 643 tare tons, and probably 710 tons gross, Finsbury Park was passed in the remarkable time of 5 minutes 58 seconds from the dead start. The driver, Lynch, of Kings Cross, was most enthusiastic about the engine, and Professor Waterhouse noted that he got this big train under way without any slipping. From the driver's subsequent remarks, No 10000 appears to have been worked pretty hard, with full regulator and full forward gear maintained right out to Holloway summit; at this point cut-off was reduced to 40 per cent.

This feat, fine though it is, and markedly superior to any 'A4' start yet published, does not, however, generally alter my contention that No 10000 is unlikely to develop, in continuous high-speed steaming, an effort superior to the 'A4s' to a degree proportionate to her greater nominal tractive effort. In starting up the heavy grade out of Kings Cross the speed is low, and no refinements in front-end design will make up for lack of sheer strength, in the form of tractive effort. Here, No 10000 might well be expected to show a marked superiority over the 'A4s', and her recent performance fully bears out such a claim. In relation to the tractive effort of the engine, it is just about equal to the feat of the 'A1' Pacific No 4472 in taking a 530-ton train through Finsbury Park in 6 minutes 10 seconds. The ratio of load to nominal tractive effort is 39.7 for the 'A1' and 38.3 for No 10000, and this slight advantage in favour of the Pacific is balanced by the fractionally

higher speed of the 4-6-4.

This start out of Kings Cross by No 10000, impressive as it is from the point of view of acceleration under arduous conditions, does not provide a real measure of the improvement in front-end efficiency realised during the Gresley regime. Reverting to the oft-quoted performance of the 'A4' No 4901, then named *Capercaillie*, between Northallerton and York, the drawbar horsepower, in relation to the nominal tractive effort, provides a striking comparison with the best I have seen with an 'A1' over this stretch, as shown in the following table:

The last of the 'A4s', No 4903, then named *Peregrine*, on the up Yorkshire Pullman near Barkstone. (*M.W. Earley*)

Engine No	4472	4901
Class	'A1'	'A4'
Load (tons, gross)	565	730
Average speed, Otterington-Poppleton Junction (mph)	72.4	75.9
Drawbar horsepower sustained for 26 miles	1,400	2,100
Ratio of dhp to nominal tractive effort	.0469	.0592

The 25 per cent superiority in favour of the 'A4' is an increase in efficiency all the more remarkable in that the 'A1' performance quoted took place when No 4472 was in her prime (after the fitting of long-travel valves). To equal the feat of *Capercaillie*, No 10000 would require to make the same speed with a load of 850 tons. Actually, the highest dhp I can find relating to No 10000 is 2,033—a speed of 85½ mph on the level with 490 tons; this is beaten by one of 2,160 by an 'A4' in comparable conditions of speed, though with a heavier load. In some correspondence concerning the work of No 10000, Mr R.A.H. Weight refers to a run on which 10000 averaged 44 mph from Hitchin up the 1 in 200 to Stevenage with a 700-ton load; the dhp involved in this case was only 1,603, whereas I have noted outputs of 1,725 dhp by 'A4s' up this same incline.

Mr Weight recalls the consternation caused among LNER enthusiasts during the locomotive exchange of 1925 when the GWR 4-6-0 No 4079 *Pendennis Castle* regularly took the test trains of 470 to 480 tons through Finsbury Park in less than 6 minutes. For a 79¾ ton locomotive hauling, if the tender is included with the train 6½ times its own weight, this was certainly a remarkable performance in 1925. The recent performance of 4-6-4 No 10000, in which roughly the same time was made with a 710-ton load, certainly serves to show the striking advance in British locomotive power since 1925. On this run the engine was hauling 7¼ times its own weight, but although showing thus a certain measure of superiority over the GWR 'Castle', No 10000 represents a very considerable advance in nominal tractive power over the Pacifics of 1925. She is only 15 per cent heavier than an 'A1', 107 against 92½ tons, and yet she develops a tractive effort greater by no less than 39 per cent! It is this attribute that is proving so useful in starting of heavy trains under conditions like those existing between Kings Cross and Finsbury Park.

Conclusion, 1937-41

In the autumn of 1937 yet another special express train service, the East Anglian, was introduced. The booked speed, however, cannot have been much to Gresley's liking, for the timings of 80 minutes for the 68.9 miles between Liverpool Street and Ipswich, and 51 minutes for the 46.2 miles on to Norwich, were no faster than some already in force—trains, moreover, of considerably greater weight than the luxurious six-coach set, taring 219 tons, built specially for the East Anglian service. A much faster schedule was at one time contemplated, but unfortunately it was found impossible, because of the density of traffic, to arrange suitable high-speed paths without providing extra track facilities. So far as locomotive power alone was concerned, it should have been easily possible with 'Sandringham' class engines to do London-Ipswich in 65 minutes, and Ipswich-Norwich in 45 minutes. Nevertheless, two of the class were specially allocated to the service, and streamlined after the style of the 'A4' Pacifics. These two engines, originally No 2859 *Norwich City* and 2870 *Manchester City*, were renamed *East Anglian* and *City of London* respectively; the latter took the title previously borne by the ex-GCR two-cylinder 4-6-0 No 5427, of the 'Sir Sam Fay' class. Both the streamlined 'B17s' have now had the valances below the running plate cut away, to give easier access to the motion.

'Sandringham' class three-cylinder 4-6-0 No 2859, previously named *Norwich City*, as rebuilt with a streamlined front end and named *East Anglian* for working the new express of that name introduced in 1937. (*British Railways*)

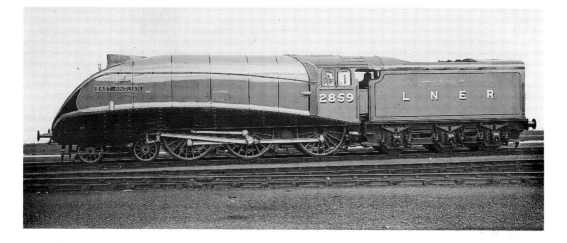

The second streamlined 'Sandringham', No 2870, formerly *Manchester City* but renamed *City of London*, working the 3.17 pm express from Ipswich to Liverpool Street on Ipswich water troughs. (*George R. Grigs*)

With the locomotives for the East Anglian service we come to the end of Gresley's express passenger designs; but before concluding the story with the two remarkable mixed-traffic classes, 'K4' and 'V4', mention must be made of the rebuilding of three locomotives, all isolated examples, yet each one significant of the general trend in LNER practice towards the end of Gresley's chieftainship. First, in 1936, one of the celebrated ex-NER 4-4-0s of Class 'R' (LNER Class 'D20') was fitted with long-travel valves. This reconstruction was considerably less extensive than that previously carried out on the 'Claud Hamiltons', for on engine No 2020 the original boiler, and—more suprisingly—the original chimney and dome were retained. The alteration to the motion was as follows:

	Original NER Class 'R'	LNER 'D20' rebuilt
Piston valve diameter (in)	8¾	10
Lap (in)	1⅛	1⅝
Travel in full gear (in)	4³/32	6

The outward appearance of No 2020 was changed somewhat by the seemingly inevitable raising of the running-plate, and as the upward curve took place in front of the leading splasher the effect was not pleasing. So far, No 2020 is the only engine of the class to be altered, but the new arrangement of the motion should enhance the excellent reputation of the 'D20s' for high-speed running with moderate loads.

After this came the rebuilding of an ex-NER Class 'S3' three-cylinder mixed-traffic 4-6-0. Engines of this class, now LNER Class 'B16', have three sets of Stephenson link motion, but in 1938 No 2364 was fitted with new cylinders, Walschaerts gear for the outside cylinders, and the Gresley derived motion for the inside cylinder. Piston-valves of 9 inches diameter, which had a travel of 6 inches at the maximum cut-off of 68 per cent, were used. This rebuilding was carried out at Darlington works, and as with the 'D20' the original North Eastern boiler, chimney and dome were retained. No 2364 in her modified form, classified 'B16/2', proved a great success and since 1929 the following engines of the 'B16' class have been similarly converted: Nos 846, 926, 1372, 1374, 2366 and 2367.

The last rebuilding to be mentioned was that of the four-cylinder Ivatt Atlantic No 3279, briefly referred to in Chapter Two. In 1938 this engine was reconstructed as a two-cylinder machine with 20 inch × 26 inch cylinders and outside Walschaerts gear. The cylinders and valves were similar to those of the 'K2' Moguls, but although the 2-6-0s and the rebuilt 4-4-2 No 3279 had 10 inch diameter piston-valves, the Atlantic had long laps and a valve travel in full gear of 6 inches against the $5^9/_{32}$ inch of the Moguls. It would be interesting to see whether No 3279 with her modern front end could equal or eclipse the maximum efforts of the standard '251' class engines. She was stationed at New England, and up to the outbreak of war there had been no recorded instance of her having to take over at a moment's notice the haulage of a 550-ton East Coast express, as the Grantham 'C1s' did on certain memorable occasions.

Mention of the 'K2' Moguls brings me to the West Highland line, and to the special 2-6-0s designed by Gresley to deal with the severe operating conditions obtaining there. Hitherto, the maximum load permitted without a pilot had been 220 tons, and winter and summer alike a good deal of double-heading was necessary. In preparing a new locomotive design for this road Gresley was handicapped not only by limitations on axle-loading but also by the curvature; but by the use of coupled wheels of only 5ft 2 in diameter, an engine of high tractive effort was produced. This was classed 'K4', and the leading dimensions make an interesting comparison with those of previous Moguls for the GNR and LNER.

Comparative dimensions of LNER Moguls

Class	'K1'	'K2'	'K3'	'K4'
Cylinders (in)	(2) 20 × 26	(2) 20 × 26	(3) 18½ × 26	(3) 18½ × 26
Coupled wheels dia (ft in)	5 8	5 8	5 8	5 2
Boiler pressure (lb/sq in)	170	170	180	200
Boiler dia (ft in)	4 8	5 6	6 0	5 6
Heating surface (sq ft):				
Small tubes	687	1,131	1,192	871
Large tubes	294	396	527	382
Firebox	137	152	182	168
Total	1,118	1,679	1,901	1,421
Superheating surface (sq ft)	303	305	407	310
Grate area	24.5	24.5	28.0	27.5
Nominal tractive effort at 85 per cent boiler pressure (lb)	22,070	22,070	30,031	36,600

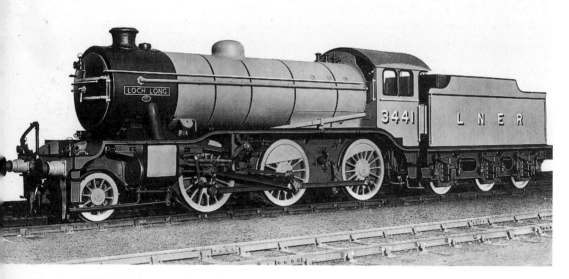

The first 'K4' 2-6-0, No 3441 *Loch Long* (British Railways)

The cylinders of the new class were the same as those of the 'K3s', but the heaviest demands for steam would be intermittent, and in any case at low speed, so that a smaller boiler could be used. This latter is outwardly of 'K2' proportions, though having considerably less evaporative heating surface. In the 'K2s', however, the large area is due mainly to the use of unusually small tubes, only 1¼ in diameter against 1¾ in tubes used in the 'K1', 'K3' and 'K4' classes; for a given smokebox vacuum, the 'K4' boiler would steam far more readily than the 'K2'. When first put into service, in the early summer of 1937, the pioneer 'K4', No 3441 *Loch Long*, was working at a boiler pressure of 180 lb sq in. After a short time this was increased to 200 lb per sq in, and with the latter the engine

Class 'K2' 2-6-0 No 4692 at Mallaig, adapted for use on the West Highland line and named *Loch Eil* (O.S. Nock)

was able to take loads up to 300 tare tons. Due to weight restrictions piloting is not permitted with the 'K4s'.

Loch Long proved a marked success, not only taking her rostered maximum load with ease, but doing so on no greater water consumption than that of the 'K2s' when hauling their 220-trains. In making the through run from Glasgow to Fort William, or vice-versa, water is normally taken only once intermediately, at Crianlarich, even with the full 300-ton load, whereas, in my experience, on up journeys with 'K2s' loaded up to, or near, their maximum load of 220 tons, a special stop at times has been necessary at Bridge of Orchy for water; and the 'K4s' have no more water capacity in their tenders than the 'K2s'. With No 3441 *Loch Long* I had

Class 'K2' 2-6-0 No 4692 *Loch Eil* leaving Glenfinnan viaduct with the afternoon up express from Mallaig. (*O.S. Nock*)

Glass 'K2' 2-6-0 No 61789 (new numbering) *Loch Laidon* on a train of fish empties for Mallaig near Banavie. (*Author's collection*)

a very interesting journey on the 5.45 am from Glasgow to Fort William, details of which are given in the accompanying table. It was an impressive experience on the footplate, and one appreciated particularly how serious is the handicap imposed by the incessant curvature, as revealed by the cut-offs used. On the Ardlui-Crianlarich and Crianlarich-Tyndrum sections—both very winding—cut-off was 32 per cent on the 1 in 60 gradients; north of Bridge of Orchy, however, we made faster climbing on a bank

LNER Dumbarton-Fort William

Engine: 'K4' 2-6-0 No 3441 *Loch Long*
Load: 286 tons tare, 305 tons full
Driver J. Thompson; Fireman G. Paterson (Fort William Shed)

Dist (miles)		Schedule (min)	Actual (min sec)	Speed (mph)	Cut-off (per cent)	Boiler pressure (lb per sq in)	Steam chest pressure (lb per sq in)
0.0	Dumbarton	0	0 00	—	65	—	—
	Cardross	—	5 50	57	22	195	185
7.1	Craigendoran Junc	—	9 43	*15	40	—	—
		—	—	21		185	175
9.3 / 0.0	Upper Helensburgh	— / 0	15 30 / 0 00	—	65	—	—
6.9	Garelochhead	—	12 10	*20	32	200	185
8.2	Milepost 10	—	14 37	—	—	200	190
8.6	Whistlefield	—	15 39	25	37	—	—
9.2	Milepost 11	—	17 28	21½	40	—	—
10.2	Milepost 12	—	20 17	20½	—	190	180
12.2	Milepost 14	—	23 48	38	32	—	—
13.5	Glen Douglas	—	25 52	—	45	—	—
		—	—	—	45	195	10
17.5 / 0.0	Arrochar	34 / 0	33 12 / 0 00	—			
8.0 / 0.0	Ardlui	15 / 0	13 50 / 0 00	—	65	—	—
0.4	Milepost 28	—	1 42	—	40	190	180
1.4	Milepost 29	—	3 55	26	32	—	—
2.4	Milepost 30	—	6 17	25	32	—	—
3.4	Milepost 31	—	8 25	33½	32	187	175
5.4	Milepost 33	—	12 30	27	32	—	—
7.4	Milepost 35	—	17 03	25½	32	190	190
8.7 / 0.0	Crianlarich	20 / 0	19 47 / 0 00	—	65	—	—
0.7	Milepost 37	—	1 45	39	32	195	185
2.7	Milepost 39	—	5 23	31	32	—	—
4.7	Milepost 41	—	10 15	23½	35	195	185
5.0 / 0.0	Tyndrum	11 / 0	11 20 / 0 00	—	65	—	—
0.7	Milepost 42	—	2 35	—	65	190	175
1.7	Milepost 43	—	4 56	28½	45	—	—
		—	—	—	45	—	—
7.5 / 0.0	Bridge of Orchy	14 / 0	14 30 / 0 00	—	65	—	—
1.2	Milepost 50	—	3 19	29	30	200	190
3.2	Milepost 52	—	6 22	44½	25	185	175
5.2	Milepost 54	—	9 46	28½	27	—	—
7.2	Milepost 56	—	13 52	31½	27	190	180
8.7	Gorton	—	16 29	36	27	—	—
15.6 / 0.0	Rannoch	27 / 0	27 12 / 0 00	—	—	—	—
1.6	Milepost 66	—	5 17	18	35	195	185
7.3	Corrour	15	15 22	—	—	—	—

* Service slack

nearly as steep though fairly straight, on but 27 per cent cut-off. Both these cut-offs are in striking contrast to the percentages of 45, 50 and even 60 per cent needed with the 'K2s' in the haulage of 220-ton loads. After the successful début of No 3441 *Loch Long,* five more of the class were constructed, like No 3441, at Darlington works, and put into service in 1938-9. These latter were painted in passenger colours and received fine Scottish names:

3442 *The Great Marquess*	3444 *Mac Calein Mor*
3443 *Cameron of Locheil*	3445 *Lord of the Isles*
3446 *Macleod of Macleod*	

The completion of what proved to be Gresley's last design was considerably delayed by the outbreak of war. Although by 1939

Class 'K4' 2-6-0 No 3443 *Cameron of Lochiel* in green livery, on an up goods train at Crianlarich. (*O.S. Nock*)

'K4' class 2-6-0 No 3446 *MacLeod of MacLeod* in green livery. (*British Railways*)

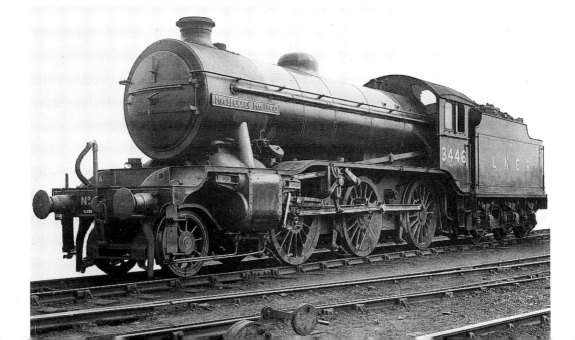

'K4' class 2-6-0 No 61995 *Cameron of Locheil* (BR numbering) on the 4.50 pm Fort William-Mallaig train, with Ben Nevis as an impressive background (*E.D. Bruton*)

a sufficient number of powerful modern locomotives had been built to cover practically all main-line requirements of the LNER, a need was expressed for a general utility design, with a fairly high nominal tractive effort, yet at the same time with a sufficiently light axle-loading to premit working over sections where the existing heavy main-line engines were not allowed to run. In adopting a maximum axle-load of 17 tons in the new 'V4' class, Gresley produced a locomotive that could be used over a total of 5,000 route miles, nearly five-sixths of the entire LNER system. The use of the 2-6-2 wheel arrangement has led to the 'V4' engines being referred to sometimes as smaller versions of the 'Green Arrows'; actually the general characteristics of the two designs differ considerably. Although the factor of adhesion is roughly the same in both cases, the boiler and firebox of the 'V2' are much larger in relation to the nominal tractive effort than in the 'V4', which was designed to put forth a high drawbar pull for short periods rather than to sustain a big effort continuously. The following are the leading dimensions of the pioneer 'V4', No 3401 *Bantam Cock*; cylinders (three) 15 in diameter by 26 in stroke; coupled wheels 5 ft 8 in diameter; total heating surface 1,799.9 sq ft; grate area 28.7 sq ft; boiler pressure 250 lb per sq in; nominal tractive effort at 85 per cent of working pressure 27,420 lb; total weight in working order (engine only) 70½ tons.

A second locomotive of the 'V4' class was completed shortly after No 3401, and it seemed that these two were forerunners of yet another numerous Gresley class. As in the case of the first two 2-8-2 express engines of Class 'P2', there were certain differences in the design of Nos 3401 and 3402, the relative merits of which were to be investigated. No 3401 had a copper firebox—a miniature edition of the standard LNER wide type as used on the

Pacifics, 2-6-2s and 2-8-2s; on No 3402 a box of similar proportions was fitted, though built in steel and of completely welded construction. In view of their widespread use abroad, the trial of steel fireboxes on the LNER was in itself a most interesting development, and the firebox of No 3402 was in addition fitted with a thermic syphon. After some experimental running in East Anglia, during which, as Mr Wethersett's photograph shows, she pulled some very heavy loads, *Bantam Cock* has joined No 3402 in Scotland. The latter engine has been working on the West Highland line, though, as might be expected, with her lesser tractive effort she was not able to tackle loads of 'K4' magnitude; the maximum rostered load for a 'V4' is 250 tons or 50 tons less than a 'K4'.

It is a little early yet to attempt to assess Grelsey's work in relation to the general development of British locomotive design. At the close of a long career, a career which towards its end was packed with stirring achievements, one naturally tends to make comparisons with the great ones of the past—with Daniel Gooch,

The first Gresley 'V4' 2-6-2, No 3401 *Bantam Cock*, on an up East Anglian express on the Cambridge line. (*E.R. Wethersett*)

The second 'V4' 2-6-2, No 3402, in 1941, with wartime shields over the cab and footplate. (*British Railways*)

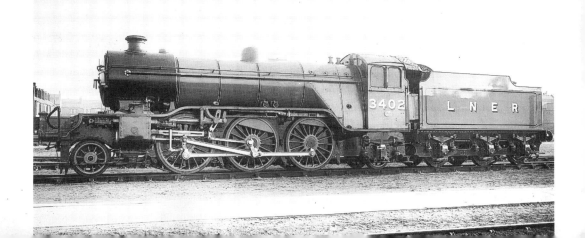

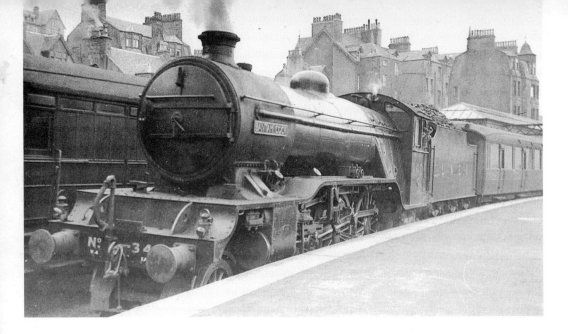

Bantam Cock on a Fort William to Glasgow express, when stationed at Eastfield, before leaving Fort William. (*O.S. Nock*)

J.F. McIntosh, Patrick Stirling, and others. Gresley was pioneering no less than they, but time alone will show whether or not he was the greatest of them all. It cannot be disputed that he put on the road, in this age of intense workings, a stud of locomotives the swiftness and reliability of which are second to none. His guiding principle of three-cylinder propulsion, with derived valve gear for the inside cylinder, may not be above criticism on theoretical grounds, but it proved remarkably effective in service. A lasting impression of footplate journeys on many locomotives of the generic Gresley three-cylinder design is of the success with which true expansive working has been made a regular everyday habit with enginemen. No driver on one of these engines, whether it was a 2-6-2 tank, a Mogul or a streamlined Pacific, would seem to think of working with anything but a wide open regulator; with this, 15 to 20 per cent cut-off has been sufficient to maintain the fastest schedules, save on the heaviest grades. All the Gresley types, too, seem very sensitive to small changes in cut-off.

Confidence in their engines has bred, all over the LNER system, a generation of drivers prepared to run hard when occasion has demanded. To some it has been second nature; to others, like the 'Geordie' who after his first, and very successful, trip with the Coronation, remarked to me, 'It's a daft train to work', it was an acquired art. A Haymarket driver, who had graduated on no faster speedway than the Edinburgh-Glasgow main line, has been timed once at 100 mph, and again at 99 mph on the down Coronation north of Newcastle. These achievements were not, as might be supposed, down the Cockburnspath bank, but between Belford and Beal, and on both occasions the full summer load was being carried. The '100' was a piece of *joie de vivre* in the course of a timekeeping journey with an 'A4', No 4486 *Merlin*, but the '99' was with an 'A3', No 2744 *Grand Parade*, on a magnificent trip when over 10 minutes of lost time were regained between Newark and Edinburgh, nearly 6 minutes of which was between Newcastle and Dunbar alone. No 2744 had come on to the train at Grantham after the booked 'A4' had failed earlier in the run. Hard running is not a recently acquired art on the Great Central section, but, having due regard to the comparative size and weight of the various GC engines in relation to the 'Sandringhams', even a Leicester driver might well be daunted at the prospect of taking a 465-ton load to Marylebone with an unpiloted 'Sandringham' on a 56.7 mph booking, when 300-320 tons was about the outside limit for 'Directors' and the Robinson 4-6-0s. Yet as recorded in the December 1939 instalment of 'British Locomotive Practice and Performance', it was done, magnificently. No 2848 *Arsenal* was the engine and, with Driver Webb at the regulator, the 103.1 miles from Leicester to Marylebone took 110 minutes 6 seconds, and the net time was exactly the 109 minutes booked.

No mention of hard running would be complete without a reference to those amazing occasions when 'C1' Atlantics took over at a moment's notice the haulage of the 1.20 pm Scotsman at Grantham. On one of these occasions, Mr Cecil J. Allen was a passenger by the train, and the wonderful feat of the North Eastern crew that took charge of engine No 4404 duly received the tremendous publicity it deserved.* But it is not generally known that this feat was closely approached on *two* other occasions! No 4404 had to tackle a colossal load of 585 tons, and yet after a slow start of 17 minutes 23 seconds to Newark passed Chaloners Whin Junction, 80.7 miles, in 83 minutes 9 seconds. Net time to York was 86½ minutes. On a second occasion, No 4415 was the engine with a load of 540 tons, and with a clear road throughout York was reached in 86 minutes 56 seconds from Grantham. Lastly, in February 1938, No 3285 was commandeered in similar circumstances, and again with a load of 540 tons made the run in 89 minutes, in spite of a long slack for permanent way repairs, costing about 3 to 3½ minutes. The three drivers concerned were Walker (Gateshead shed) on No 4404; Samwells (Kings Cross shed) on No 4415; and Peachey (Kings Cross shed) on No 3285. Their magnificent running in these three emergencies provides some outstanding examples of the capabilities of the 'C1' Atlantics that incorporate the Gresley modifications described in Chapter Two.

Although Gresley was above all else a practical engineer, who was usually ahead rather than abreast of the times, he had a strongly developed perception of the historical background of railway locomotion. His affection for the only surviving Stirling '8-

---

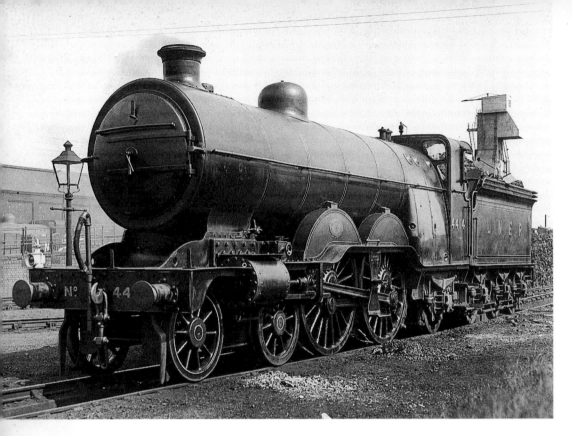

One of the famous large-boilered GNR Atlantics, No 4414, on shed at Grantham in 1938. (*Rail Archive Stephenson, T.G. Hepburn*)

footer' was known only by a very few, until, to commemorate the fiftieth anniversary of the first Race of the North, and to introduce the 1938 rolling-stock for the Flying Scotsman, it was suggested that she be brought out of York Museum to run again. Once the idea was put to him there was no one keener on the project; and in all the preparation of No 1 for the road he took a deep personal interest. This running of No 1 in 1938 was, of course, pure pageantry, but there was an occasion eight years earlier when Gresley put an 8-foot single design to practical use. The experimental 4-6-4 No 10000 was on trial, and steaming badly. Gresley admitted he was nonplussed, and then surprised those immediately concerned by asking for a general arrangement drawing of the final batch of Stirling 8-footers to be obtained from Doncaster, remarking at the same time that 'those engines steamed all right, yet they had no boiler to speak of!' The drawing was duly studied, and as a result the blast-pipe of his giant 4-6-4 was entirely remodelled on the lines of that fitted to the 1003-8 class of 8-footers. It was in this modified condition that the original No 10000 did all her best running.

Nowadays it seems a far cry from the Stirling 8-footers to No 10000; though not quite the alpha and omega of East Coast locomotive history, they are sufficiently apart to emphasise the profound changes that have taken place during Gresley's career. When he succeeded Ivatt the 8-footers were still working in express passenger service, and it is pleasing to realise that his experience

of their working was not pushed aside and forgotten amidst a welter of modern problems. That Gresley in the flood tide of almost unbroken success could, when in a particular difficulty, turn for inspiration to a Stirling design, is indeed a mark of his greatness, the greatness that made his chieftainship one of the most fruitful in British railway history.

While it is as a locomotive engineer that Gresley will be best remembered, locomotives formed but a part, albeit the most spectacular part of his life's work. Not only was he responsible also for carriages, wagons and all the other ramifications of the Chief Mechanical Engineer's department, but also for the electrical engineering. The electrification of the Manchester-Sheffield line was planned under his direction, and he was responsible, jointly with the Civil Engineer of the Southern Area of the LNER, for the equipment of the first fully-mechanised hump marshalling yard in this country, at Whitemoor, near March. Although this book has been concerned solely with his locomotives, this brief reference to the full extent of his vast responsibilities may help towards a truer appreciation of the stature of the man himself.

His responsibilities were shouldered through a period of unexampled difficulty. In 1914 the nation had no conception of what war on the grand scale was going to involve; yet during that period, when the Great Northern Railway, like every other line in the country, was profoundly affected, some major points in his future locomotive policy were developed. The immediate post-

The famous Stirling 8-foot single No 1 in the old Railway Museum at York before her emergence as a working engine once more in 1938. (*O.S. Nock*)

145

Sir Nigel off duty.
(*British Railways*)

war period was one of uncertainty, pending Parliamentary decisions on the future of British railways as a whole, and then came his task of integrating the technical staffs of the constituent companies of the LNER into one team. Trade depression, the great slump and the subsequent period of intense effort by the railways to regain lost traffic stimulated technical advances and led to the brilliant achievements of his locomotives during the third decade of his career.

Sir Nigel Gresley died on 5 April, 1941, at Watton House, Hert-

The naming ceremony of No 4498 *Sir Nigel Gresley* at Marylebone, 26 November 1937; LNER Chairman William Whitelaw unveils the nameplate. (*British Railways*)

ford, and thus his great career came to a premature end. It was a career that brought him many honours. In January 1920 he was awarded the CBE for special services rendered during the war of 1914-19; in the Birthday Honours of 1936 he was created a Knight Bachelor. The University of Manchester also in 1936 conferred upon him the Honorary Degree of Doctor of Science, but it was

Gresley and his staff after the ceremony:
1 B. Spencer
2 D.R. Edge
3 A.H. Peppercorn
4 F. Wintour
5 R.A. Thom
6 O.V.S. Bulleid
7 F.H. Eggleshaw
8 E. Thompson
(*British Railways*)

from his own company that he received the rarest distinction of all. On 26 November, 1937, the nameplates of his hundredth Pacific were unveiled by Mr William Whitelaw, Chairman of LNER, in a ceremony at Marylebone station. This engine, No 4498, was named *Sir Nigel Gresley*.

Many famous locomotive engineers have in the past been honoured after either their retirement, or their death, by having a locomotive named after them; it is, therefore, significant of the heights of achievement which Gresley attained that this honour should have been conferred upon him while he was still in harness. In a happy speech at the naming ceremony, Mr Whitelaw referred to engine No 4498 as one of the most beautiful examples of locomotive engineering that the world knew, and to Sir Nigel himself as occupying a foremost position in the whole world of mechanical engineering. Gresley was indeed a great engineer, but he was something greater still, he was a great railwayman.

An indeterminate period, 1941-48

It is no disparagement to the memory of those who followed him to say that the death of Sir Nigel Gresley left a profound gap in the ranks of LNER senior officers. He had been a man of towering structure. His locomotives had brought world-wide fame to his railway, to such an extent that one is apt to forget that from the shareholders' point of view the LNER was the least attractive of all the British railways during the grouping era. Yet such were the achievements of the Gresley locomotives that everyone concerned with the line, right down to the humblest country porter, delighted to bask in the glow that emanated from the daily work of the 'A4s', let alone such a breathtaking feat as that of *Mallard*.

Edward Thompson was appointed to succeed Gresley at a very anxious and critical stage of the Second World War, and the new Chief once told me personally how at the time he was appointed, the Chairman, Sir Ronald Matthews, told him that there was no need to spend time designing new engines, that Gresley's were unbeatable, and if more were needed he was just to use the existing designs. Matthews got the shock of his life when Thompson's

The wartime Flying Scotsman with a scruffy out-of-condition 'A4' No 4482 *Golden Eagle*, in unlined black with 'NE' on the tender, working through from Peterborough to Newcastle, seen here leaving York with the author on the footplate. (*W. Hubert Foster*)

A Canal (Carlisle)-based 'A3', No 2747 *Coronach*, on the Waverley route connection off the morning Midland train from Leeds, on which the author rode through to Edinburgh. (*O.S. Nock*)

reply amounted virtually to 'over my dead body'!

A long discussion followed, during which Thompson went to great lengths to explain the difficulties that were being experienced with engines having the three-cylinder conjugated valve gear. Sir Ronald was incredulous, and eventually Thompson made a characteristic gesture. In as many words he said: 'If you don't believe me, get an independent authority to examine the position. If I'm wrong my office is at your disposal; if I'm right I require your consent to make radical changes.' Again Sir Ronald was incredulous, and asked if Thompson was really prepared to invite some outsider to examine all the confidential works and drawing office reports, and make an independent assessment—particularly on the position appertaining to engines fitted with the conjugated valve gear. The latter was of course the very cornerstone of Gresley's designs, both large and small, and to condemn it was to condemn most of what Gresley had done in the past 20-odd years. But Thompson persisted, and eventually Sir Ronald Matthews agreed to his seeking an independent arbitrator.

The question was, who? It must clearly be an engineer of the very highest status, and I believe that Thompson first approached Bulleid, as being an engineer very closely associated with Sir Nigel Gresley over many years. But 'OVSB' was one of his staunchest lieutenants, and I can quite believe that he would have nothing to do with the proposals that Thompson was making. So Thompson approached Sir William Stanier who at that time was away

A deplorably dirty 'A4', No 60002 *Sir Murrough Wilson* (new name), crossing the King Edward bridge, Newcastle, with the up Flying Scotsman. (*S.E. Teasdale*)

from the LMS, and seconded for special Governmental duties in connection with the war. Thompson told me how he put his difficulties to Sir William, and how eventually Stanier agreed to make the investigation. Although Thompson confided many details of his early months to me, he did not show me a copy of the report. I gathered it was couched in rather non-committal terms. Stanier did not condemn the three-cylinder conjugated valve gear as such, and went no further than to say that he would not use it himself. As Stanier had built many three-cylinder engines for the LMS this could be taken as a reflection on the Gresley arrangement, though really no more than a vaguely indirect one. But it was enough to secure for Thompson the necessary authority to discard it in all new designs for the LNER.

Thompson decided to build the prototype of his new standard Pacific design by rebuilding an existing engine. Gresley's mighty 'P2' Mikados were only six in number. Under the stress of wartime conditions, and in deteriorating standards of maintenance, they were reputed to be giving trouble on the Aberdeen route; though what had happened to them since I made my footplate journeys I cannot imagine. As I remarked in an earlier chapter of this book, I found them truly superb locomotives. Having the somewhat discredited conjugated valve gear, they provided a ready-made set of 'guinea pigs' for Thompson's new programme, and in 1943 engine No 2006 *Wolf of Badenoch* was rebuilt as a Pacific. By removing the leading pair of coupled wheels, fitting new cylinders and motion, and substituting a leading bogie for the pony truck, a prototype Pacific was quite ingeniously produced without any alteration to the length of the frame. The boiler remained unchanged, though the striking streamlined front casing was removed.

Although the prototype had been produced incorporating three sets of valve gear, and equal length of connecting rods for all three cylinders, the engine looked a horrible makeshift, with an inordinate distance between the rear bogie wheel and the leading pair of coupled wheels. In comparison to the beautifully proportioned designs of Sir Nigel Gresley the rebuild was not 'easy on the eye', quite apart from the surprise and shock the rebuilding itself imparted to admirers of Gresley's work. Onlookers from outside, of course, had no conception of what had gone on behind the scenes of the LNER since Thompson's appointment, and while failure of the conjugated valve gear had been known in pre-war years, the official announcement that the rebuilding was due to unsatisfactory performance on the Aberdeen road did not have a very convincing ring about it. Surely, it was argued, ample use could have been made of six such powerful engines south of Edinburgh, if it was the curves that were causing heavy maintenance costs. Wartime loads on the East Coast route were of gargantuan proportions, sometimes requiring the double-heading even of Pacifics on the Cockburnspath bank. One can pass over the vapourings of the 'lunatic fringe' of LNER fans, who averred that to alter anything that Gresley had created was an act of iconoclasm; but there is no doubt that this rebuilding of the 'P2' engines—for conversion of the five remaining ones quickly followed that of No 2006—caused much genuine astonishment among locomotive men in general.

Taking all into account, one could have accepted the makeshift rebuilt 'P2s', but it soon transpired that this curious wheel spacing was to be the new standard. The last four engines of an order for 'V2' 2-6-2s of Gresley design were built as 4-6-2s in the Thompson style, and then in 1946 there came the biggest shock of all. To provide the prototype for his new express passenger Pacific he took the pioneer Gresley Pacific No 4470 *Great Northern* and completely rebuilt it as a 6 ft 8 in version of the rebuilt 'P2' class. Now, whatever troubles may have beset them during the war years, the Gresley Pacifics as a family of engines, 'A1', 'A3' and 'A4' alike, had been an outstanding success, and to locomotive men, as well as to the large body of amateur enthusiasts, *Great Northern*, as the first engine of the family, occupied much the same place in their regard and affection as the Stirling 8-footer No 1, as the pioneer British Atlantic No 990 *Henry Oakley,* and as the ever-famous pioneer of the large-boilered Great Northern Atlantics, No 251. The pioneer Pacific No 4470 was the culmination of the Great Northern Railway saga, and many people felt that it was almost a foregone conclusion the same day she would be preserved, and exhibited alongside No 1, No 990 and No 251. Imagine, then, the consternation when she was rebuilt out of all recognition, as an addition to the stud of 'makeshifts' and, above all, painted in a royal blue livery similar to, though not quite so elaborate as, that of the Great Eastern in the days prior to the First World War.

Among locomotive lovers harsh words were used about Thompson and all his works, and comments not greatly watered down appeared in some of the enthusiast journals. Highly critical letters were published even in such journals as *The Railway Gazette*. At the time I was engaged on making a number of footplate journeys in all parts of the country in connection with a series of articles I had been commissioned to write for *The Engineer*; the scripts of those articles were in due course submitted to Thompson, and in giving his approval he invited me to visit him at Doncaster, so that he could explain to me the policy on which he had been working. It was then that I learned much of the background information contained in this particular chapter. It was no formal visit. I was invited to spend the night at his home, and it was at his own fireside that he told me of the situation regarding the conjugated valve gear, and of how he came to formulate the plan for the range of standard two-cylinder locomotives. I remember him as a charming host; a tall, elegant, scholarly man, but one who was highly sensitive, and it was the criticism of his work in the railway press that had greatly distressed him, and led to his invitation to me—with the hope that I might help to redress the situation that had arisen. He felt very strongly and sincerely about the conjugated valve gear, and the following day at Doncaster works a great amount of data had been laid out for me to examine. In the shops I saw several examples of gears that had caused the engines concerned to become total failures on the road. He ended a memorable visit with an invitation to ride on the new No 4470 *Great Northern*, which he offered to have put on to any train I liked.

Thompson's stay as Chief Mechanical Engineer was no more than brief. He retired in the autumn of 1946, and with the appointment of Arthur H. Peppercorn as his successor, and with nationalisation of the British railways imminent, his carefully worked out plan for future locomotive standardisation was to a large extent stillborn. New Pacific engines were authorised, but Peppercorn immediately discarded one of Thompson's most cherished precepts by reverting to a more normal wheel spacing, with unequal lengths of connecting rod for the outside and inside cylinders, but retaining three sets of valve gear. Thus the peculiar Thompson wheel spacing which was intended to be the future LNER standard for Pacific engines was confined to no more than 26 examples: the six rebuilt P2s, the four 'orphans of the storm,' as Thompson always called the four 'V2s' which he altered to Pacifics, the 15 new engines, Nos 500 and 511 to 524, and the unfortunate No 4470 *Great Northern*. The first new Pacific, No 500, was named *Edward Thompson* at a little ceremony presided over by Sir Ronald Matthews. It was a pleasing gesture to a man whose motives were to a great extent misunderstood, and who I feel sure acted with deep conviction. But I do wish he had chosen a different Gresley Pacific to rebuild as his prototype express passenger engine!

Although the London & North Eastern Railway itself ceased to exist from 1 January 1948, one cannot ring down the curtain abruptly upon all that happened afterwards, because in many ways the history of LNER steam locomotives in the ensuing dozen years includes many points of deep significance, particularly in relation to the design features of the Gresley locomotives. The three-cylinder engines, especially the Pacifics and the 'V2s', were still under something of a cloud at the time of nationalisation, and the reputation of the 'A4s' was not enhanced in the interchange trials of 1948, for reasons to be described later. When the project of large-scale locomotive interchange trials was first mooted, only a few weeks after nationalisation had taken place, it was originally suggested that one of the latest Pacifics should represent the Eastern and North Eastern Regions in the first-line express passenger engine trials. When it came to the final selection of locomotive, however, the two regions were not prepared to put either a Thompson or a Peppercorn Pacific into the arena, and so authority fell back upon a Gresley 'A4'.

On the first day of the 1948 Interchange Trials, 26 April: *Mallard* in garter blue leaving Paddington with the 1.30 pm West of England express in the week of preliminary running. (*C.E.B. Herbert*)

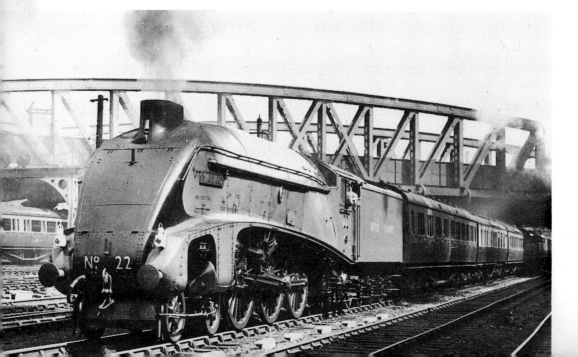

For these famous engines it could have been a resounding triumph; a vindication of the design, sweeping aside all the doubts and denigrations that had followed the death of Sir Nigel Gresley. Unfortunately, high authority, authority that was not in touch with day-to-day running affairs, insisted that the regions' representative should be the historic world record breaker *Mallard*. Unfortunately that engine was far from being in good condition at the time, and those responsible at Kings Cross 'Top Shed' pleaded incessantly against this directive. But *Mallard* it had to be, and as those who knew best had feared, she failed on the Western Region even before the preliminary running had been completed. *Seagull* was substituted, and she failed in tests on the Southern Region. *Mallard* took up the running again, and failed a second time; and so a third 'A4' had to be used to finish the tests, No 60034 *Lord Faringdon*.

The drivers, knowing only too well that they had engines below standard, handled them with the utmost care and skill, and one rarely saw the fire and dash that had characterised 'A4' performance in former days. As it turned out, these engines had the lowest basic coal consumption of any of the large express passenger classes; but much of it was achieved by running that could not be called anything but mediocre when the work of these engines in pre-war years was recalled. Some observers felt that the 'A4s' had passed their prime and could no longer repeat their pre-war feats; but only a few weeks after the conclusion of the interchange trials I rode No 60030 *Golden Fleece* from Kings Cross to Grantham and recorded some magnificent running, quite up to the old standards. For the record I have tabulated one interest-

Later the same week, after *Mallard* had failed, another 'A4', No 60033 *Seagull*, on the same service leaving Reading. (*M.W. Earley*)

Southern Region: Salisbury-Exeter (1948 Interchange Trials)

Engine: Class 'A4' 4-6-2 No 22 *Mallard*
Load: 481 tons tare, 505 tons full

Dist (miles)		Schedule (min)	Actual (min sec)	Speeds (mph)
0.0	SALISBURY	0	0 00	—
2.5	Wilton		5 08	—
8.2	Dinton		11 25	—
12.5	Tisbury		15 47	—
17.5	Semley		21 13	48
21.6	Gillingham		25 06	69
23.9	Milepost 107½		27 11	58
28.4	TEMPLECOMBE	34	31 16	73
29.9	Milepost 113½		33 10	42½
34.5	Sherborne		37 40	75
39.1	YEOVIL JUNCTION	47	41 39	68½
42.7	Milepost 126¼		45 19	50
47.9	Crewkerne		50 18	66
49.7	Milepost 133¼		52 51	36
55.9	Chard Junction		58 31	76½
61.0	Axminster		62 20	82
64.2	Seaton Junction		64 48	73½
69.0	Milepost 152½		70 46	33½
70.0	Milepost 153½		72 45	30
71.2	Honiton		74 10	—
—			—	70
75.8	SIDMOUTH JUNC	90	79 24	
—			pws	—
3.7	Whimple		7 43	—
7.4	Broad Clyst		—	67½
11.1	Exmouth Junc		15 07	
12.2	EXETER	16	18 11	

ing run made by an 'A4' on a 'foreign' line during the interchange trials: with *Mallard* from Salisbury to Exeter. In view of the recent exploits of the now privately owned No 4498 *Sir Nigel Gresley*, it would have been extremely interesting to see what an 'A4' could have done with the 530-ton test trains between Crewe and Carlisle, had the schedules been smart and the line free from checks. But the schedule time of the down Royal Scot then allowed as much as 183 minutes for the 141 miles from Crewe to Carlisle, and so many speed restrictions were in force for track repairs that on one occasion the 'A4' Pacific No 60034 *Lord Faringdon* took 203 minutes for the trip!

The main line of the Southern, and particularly that west of Salisbury, had been little affected by the maintenance difficulties that had beset so many famous British routes in the war years and in the period of austerity that followed, and in contrast to the conditions elsewhere *Mallard* was able to run in magnificent style on the down Atlantic Coast Express. The late R.E. Charlewood gave me details of this run, and it was one of the fastest ever made over that route with such a load—a route traditionally

the scene of very fast running, from the days of Dugald Drummond on the London & South Western Railway.

Because of delays east of Basingstoke the train was considerably behind time on arrival at Salisbury, but with the wholehearted support of the Southern Inspector who was riding on the footplate, the Kings Cross driver gave *Mallard* her head from Salisbury onwards. Apart from clocking the notable minimum speed of 48 mph at Semley with this 505-ton load, Charlewood did not record any speeds on the continuous rise up from Wilton, but the average speeds between the stations, 54.3 mph between Wilton and Dinton, 59.1 mph on to Tisbury, and 55 mph up the final 5 miles to Semley showed very much finer work than *Mallard*'s LMR rivals in the exchange running. After Semley both the latter engines were run at considerably higher speed downhill, though not overtaking the splendid times made by *Mallard* in her remarkable start from Salisbury up to Semley. As the log shows, the train had gained more than 5 minutes on the scheduled time from Salisbury to Yeovil Junction, and after a bracing spin down hill past Axminster there came the notable climb of the Seaton bank, with the remarkable speed of 33½ mph on entering Honiton Tunnel at milepost 152½, after ½ mile at 1 in 100, and 4½ miles at 1 in 80. There was some slight slipping in the tunnel itself, but a relatively easy descent brought the train into Sidmouth Junction 10½ minutes inside scheduled time.

But *Mallard*'s hour of glory, in 1948, was short-lived. On the up Atlantic Coast Express on the following day she failed again, and had to be taken off the train at Salisbury. What this noble engine could really do in ordinary service 15 years later is shown by the monumental performance described towards the end of the next chapter of this book.

On 8 June, *Mallard* again, on a dynamometer car run with the Atlantic Coast Express near Basingstoke. (*M.W. Earley*)

At the end of 1949 Peppercorn retired, as did his fellow CMEs of the old independent railways such as Hawksworth of the Great Western, while Bulleid had already gone over to Ireland in October of that same year. The road was then apparently clear for the boffins at 222 Marylebone Road to spread their influence nation-wide. In the meantime, however, the results of the somewhat hastily organised Locomotive Interchange Trials of 1948 had been published with many details that cannot have been to the liking of the ex-LMS men who constituted the backbone of the Railway Executive. In the group of trials involving the top link express passenger engines, the Gresley 'A4' Pacific seems to have been a rather hurried second choice, as the preliminary notices, which were published very soon after the national railway organisation was established, gave the Eastern Region participant as 'Pacific latest type'. At that time, the latest was the Peppercorn 'A2', and immediately before that the Thompson types. The latter had quickly fallen into disfavour and were not to be considered by the Eastern Region men, while the first of the Peppercorns had been introduced no more than a few months before trials were due to start. So, somewhat reluctantly on the part of the organisers at 222 Marylebone Road, the Eastern Region had to fall back on the Gresley 'A4'.

Class 'A4' 4-6-2 No 60015 *Quicksilver* in experimental dark blue livery drawing forward out of York station with a train of empty stock. (*E.D. Bruton*)

This, as we have seen, was a misfortune from the foreward planning point of view. The Gresley three-cylinder engine layout, with the conjugated gear for driving the piston-valves of the inside cylinder, had been discredited in the higher echelons of the LNER motive power department, though not among the majority of Run-

ning Inspectors. But for the seemingly precipitate haste in which the Interchange Trials were organised, there was no doubt one of the Peppercorn engines would have participated. However, when the results were published, the Gresley 'A4' Pacifics came out with the lowest coal consumption of any of the express passenger engines tested. Of course, they earned black marks from the three total failures on the road requiring the removal of the engines from their trains and consequent delays. They were the only engines that suffered thus in the whole series of trials, and naturally the blame was laid on the conjugated valve gear which was doubly damned in certain people's eyes. But one of the principal villains of the piece, though not by any means the predominating one, was the low standard of maintenance that had been allowed to develop in the later stages of the war and thereafter. There were many Gresley Pacifics in first-class fettle in 1948-49, as the runs I was privileged to make on the footplate at that time showed, but it was unfortunate that the chosen ones let the side down.

When the venturesome step was taken in the summer service of 1948 to restore non-stop running between Kings Cross and Edinburgh, although there were then many Peppercorn 'A1' Pacifics in service, and apparently winning many honours in working the train services which at that time were not very fast, none of them had been fitted with a corridor tender, so dependence for the haulage of the 'non-stop' had to remain with the Gresley 'A4s', and right royally they responded to the challenge. The restored service ran from 21 May until the afternoon of 12 August

Class 'A4' 4-6-2 No 60030 *Golden Fleece*, beautifully turned out in garter blue, in the locomotive yard at Kings Cross. (*W.J. Reynolds*)

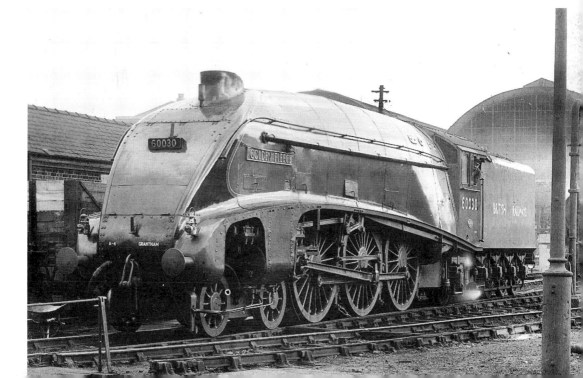

when rainstorms culminating in a cloudburst of unprecedented violence caused complete breaching of the main line between Berwick and Dunbar in no fewer than *ten* places. All through traffic was diverted from Tweedmouth Junction via Kelso and Galashiels. At first there was no thought of continuing with the Flying Scotsman as a non-stop train. Rear-end banking assistance was necessary on the southbound run from Hardengreen Junction up to Falahill, where the gradient was 1 in 70 and on which the maximum load for an unassisted Pacific was 400 tons. Also, in view of the length of the run to the first set of water troughs at Belford, 90 miles out of Edinburgh by the diversion route, it was thought advisable to take water at Galashiels. Although the route was no more than 15.9 miles longer than by the direct line via Dunbar, the heavy gradients between Portobello and St Boswells and the lengths of restricted speed between the latter junction and Tweedmouth Junction caused the overall time between Edinburgh and Kings Cross to be increased by about 70 minutes.

After no more that 12 days of this emergency working, the pride of the Scottish enginemen in the running of the 'non-stop' inspired the Haymarket crew on the up train to try to get through without any stop at all, even though they had a load of 435 tons instead of the stipulated maximum of 400; with engine No 60029 *Woodcock* they succeeded, making a new world record non-stop run of 408.6 miles. That was on 24 August 1948, and thereafter, before the summer service ended, this remarkable feat was repeated on 16 occasions, eight in each direction. *Woodcock* was very much the favourite engine on the job because it featured in no fewer than

Class 'A4' 4-6-2 No 60012 *Commonwealth of Australia* on The Capitals Limited before leaving Kings Cross. (*W.J. Reynolds*)

nine of the 16 runs made non-stop via Galashiels, five in the up direction and four going down. Others that participated were *Commonwealth of Australia* (three times) *Merlin, Sea Eagle, Golden Plover* and the historic *Mallard*. (Engine No 60028 *Sea Eagle* was afterwards renamed *Walter K Whigham*). I had no opportunity of travelling by the train on the summer service, but Scottish Region later gave me a footplate pass to ride on the southbound Flying Scotsman from Edinburgh to Tweedmouth. With the heavy winter load of 480 tons tare it was necessary to stop for a bank engine at Hardengreen Junction and also for water at Galashiels. The engine was *Merlin*, and they made a good job of it.

In the following summer, the three Regions covering the East Coast route combined to put on a new non-stop Scotsman at a considerably accelerated timing, the Capitals Limited, running half an hour ahead of the Flying Scotsman and taking 7 hr 20 min for the journey of 392.7 miles. Two years later, when I had a footplate pass to ride the down train, we had the same 'A4' that had done so well in the 1948 emergency, No 60029 *Woodcock*. However, at no time during the long run could it be said that the engine was steaming freely, but to the lasting credit of the two crews concerned they not only surmounted difficulties on the footplate but recovered all but 4¼ minutes of 29 minutes that had been lost by exceptional circumstances by the time Grantham was passed. The ensuing 287.25 miles to Edinburgh Waverley were covered in exactly 5 hours at an average speed of 57.5 mph, including two more moderate checks. It was a great run.

When Ivatt succeeded Fairburn as CME of the LMS, he initiated

The Leeds-Glasgow restaurant car express, in experimental livery, entering Newcastle hauled by Class 'A3' 4-6-2 No 60045 *Lemberg*. (*H. Gordon Tidey*)

The 12.40 pm up express from Aberdeen climbing to the Forth Bridge hauled by Class 'A3' 4-6-2 No 60057 *Ormonde*. (*E.D. Bruton*)

Flying Scotsman, the most famous of the Gresley Pacifics, modified with an 'A3' boiler and finished in the standard Brunswick green livery. (*British Railways*)

certain measures designed to improve the availability of locomotives, particularly those of the general utility type such as the Stanier 'Black Five' 4-6-0. One of these measures was the fitting of the so-called self-cleaning screens in the smokebox. Unburnt particles of fuel carried forward through the tubes were arrested by the screens and were caused to fall down to the bottom of the smokebox. It was claimed that this accumulation could then be more easily removed; in fact, the LMS engines so fitted could run for a week without their smokeboxes being opened. After nationalisation, at the regular meetings of the Regional Locomotive Engineers, the attributes of the LMS-inspired self-cleaning smokebox were no doubt discussed freely, and the Eastern Region decided to fit similar screens to some of the Gresley 'V2' 2-6-2s

in view of their general utility nature. These engines had emerged from the war years with a far better reputation than most of the Gresley three-cylinder classes, and with the departure of Edward Thompson from the Doncaster scene they were largely restored to their original fame. When a few of them were fitted with self-cleaning screens in the smokebox, however, their steaming, to use a colloquialism, was 'knocked for six'. While the standard 'V2s' were able to sustain a steaming rate of 25,000 lb easily, those with the screens inserted were not able to reach half that figure.

In the meantime, the Locomotive Testing Committee of the Railway Executive had fully settled into its stride. In this particular activity it was fortunate that the inter-railway rivalry, which had dogged the early proceedings of the Executive, had quickly ended

The Tees-Tyne Pullman at Marshmoor, hauled by Class 'A4' 4-6-2 No 60010 *Dominion of Canada* in the standard green livery. (*E.D. Bruton*)

Class 'A4' 4-6-2 No 60039 *Sandwich* in green livery at Kings Cross. (*W.J. Reynolds*)

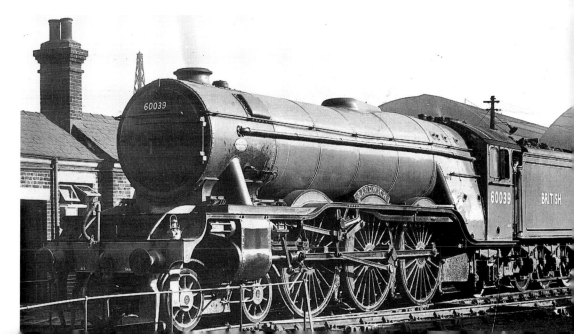

with the senior engineers at 'No 222' realising that the Swindon Stationary Testing Plant, as modernised by the Great Western Railway in the 1930s, was a magnificent tool of management. It was fully equal, in its technical potentialities, to the recently commissioned plant at Rugby, and was also backed by a wealth of experience in the testing staff which the new plant did not then possess. At the time of nationalisation, Swindon was busily engaged on tests with 'Castle' class 4-6-0s with varying degrees of superheat. These were conducted under the former GWR Drawing Office organization in which the testing staff reported to the Chief Draughtsman. When these tests were finished, further work came under the authority of the Railway Executive, and a series of tests on mixed traffic locomotives began simultaneously at Swindon and Rugby. It was quickly realised that the Swindon procedure, which was accepted by the Railway Executive and also adopted at Rugby, provided an admirable means of analysing faults and of trying out alternatives, and this was done with certain LMS-designed mixed traffic engines at Swindon.

12

Indian Summer of the Pacifics

In the summer of 1951, H.G. Ivatt, the last of the CMEs of the old privately owned railways, was due for retirement. His going would give the British Railways Chief Mechanical Engineer R.A. Riddles the opportunity he desired of doing a major exercise in cross-breeding of Regional Mechanical Engineers. Harrison, who had succeeded Peppercorn at Doncaster, was to go to Derby, K.J. Cook from Swindon, was to take charge of the Eastern and North Eastern Regions, and Alfred Smeddle, originally from the North Eastern, who, after Bulleid's departure, had been Deputy CME of the Southern, was to go to Swindon. It did not work out quite that way, at any rate so far as Doncaster, Darlington and Swindon were concerned. Cook, at first, was not at all keen on the transfer. He had been at Swindon all his life, and although his position was much diluted from that previously held by Hawksworth and his predecessors by the detachment of the Carriage and Wagon and the Locomotive Running departments, he was still sitting in the chair of Churchward, and that meant a good deal to a Great Western man. Although constrained by the circumstances of the time, he felt that there was much he could do to get the Locomotive Department back to its pre-war levels of efficiency, particularly as Keith Grand, the Chief Regional Officer, was constantly pressing for acceleration of train services.

At his new headquarters at Doncaster, Cook found the design staff in the throes of the 'V2' problem. Spencer, who had been reinstated after the departure of Thompson, had been appointed Chairman of the small sub-committee of the main Locomotive Testing Committee of the Railway Executive charged with responsibility for the detail work in testing the individual locomotives selected for examination. In his main sphere of responsibility, locomotive design at Doncaster, Spencer was much concerned with the troubles encountered on the fitting of the self-cleaning screens to the 'V2s'. He had been intimately concerned with the original design of those engines under Gresley's direction, and was well enough aware that, in spite of the wartime vicissitudes, there had not been any basic troubles with steaming up until then. He discussed the problem with Cook, his new Chief, who, Spencer confided to me some months afterwards, 'was the nicest

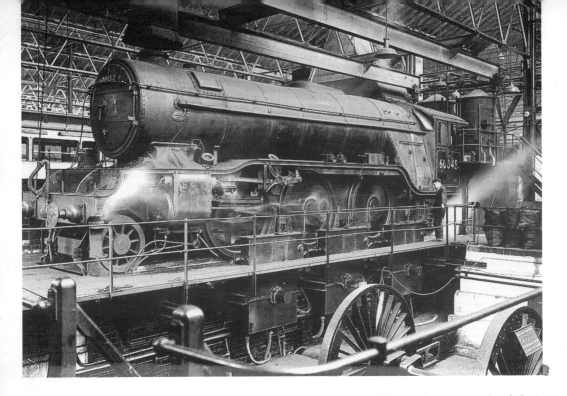

Above Class 'V2' 2-6-2 No 60845 on the Stationary Testing Plant at Swindon in 1953 (*British Railways*)

chap we've had at Doncaster since Gresley'. As a result of their efforts, arrangements were made to include one of the modified 'V2s' in the programme of locomotives to be examined on the Swindon plant. I have no information as to why Swindon was chosen instead of Rugby, except to suggest that if Cook himself had any part in making the decision one can be sure that he would have plumped heavily for his former headquarters on the dual grounds of its past record of achievement and the expertise of its current staff.

Under the masterly direction of Sam Ell, one of the most erudite of experimental engineers, the problem was soon laid bare. Having done some preliminary steaming trials on the Stationary Plant with the engine as received, confirming its dismal performance, the screens were then removed, and further trials restored normal 'V2' steaming. Then the blast arrangements were studied, and various alternatives tested, the upshot of which was that an entirely new draughting arrangement was designed. As finalized, not only was the steaming rate even with the self-cleaning screens reinserted fully restored, but, by expert firing, as was undoubtedly made on certain pre-war record runs with these engines, enhanced. I was privileged to witness some of the concluding tests on the Plant and also to ride in the famous Churchward dynamometer car on confirmatory road tests, and very impressive they were. I travelled on a day when the test load was 20 coaches, 610 tons, and saw this huge load hauled at a steady speed of 60 mph on level track.

Details were given in the Test Bulletin issued by the Railway Executive later of a performance with a still heavier load of 25 coaches totalling 761.7 tons, on which the steam rate to the cylinders was constantly maintained for the whole trial time of 69 minutes during which the average speed was exactly 60 mph. The test began when speed from the start at Stoke Gifford sidings had reached 30 mph on the rising 1 in 300 gradient. Thenceforward, the variations in speed were 43 mph attained and sustained on the continuing 1 in 300 to Badminton, 75 mph at Little Somerford, 54 mph minimum at Wootton Bassett and 70 mph sustained on the easy descending gradients, maximum 1 in 754,

Below left A controlled road test with the ex-GWR dynamometer car leaving Scours Lane sidings, west of Reading, with 'V2' engine No 60845. (*M.W. Earley*)

Above The controlled road test, with maximum load and power, passing Hullavington, with the author in the dynamometer car. (*K.H. Leech*)

167

'V2s' to the rescue of the Southern in 1953, due to temporary withdrawal of Bulleid Pacifics. Class V2 No 60917 on a Bournemouth express at Waterloo on 16 May. (*W.J. Reynolds*)

between Swindon and Didcot. The regulator was full open throughout the test, and, apart from the period of acceleration from the initial 30 mph to full running speed, the cut-offs varied from 30 per cent on the rising 1 in 300 gradient down to 22 per cent for the fast running between Swindon and Didcot. The steam rate to the cylinders was 23,950 lb per hour, showing a handsome margin in reserve from the maximum of 31,000 lb per hour attained on the Swindon Stationary Testing Plant. Cook was so pleased with the results that when the engine, No 60845, got back to Doncaster he decided to earmark it by fitting a copper-capped chimney as evidence of its stay at Swindon. Unfortunately, someone very high up at '222' objected, and he was ordered to take it off!

The year 1953, the Coronation Year of Her Majesty Queen Elizabeth II, was celebrated on British Railways in a variety of ways,

Class 'V2' 2-6-2 No 60893 on the down Bournemouth Belle Pullman car express near Basingstoke on 28 May. (*M.W. Earley*)

notably by the renaming of the East Coast non-stop London-Edinburgh express as the Elizabethan. Before coming to that splendid train, which enabled the Gresley 'A4' Pacifics to see steam out on the East Coast route in a blaze of glory, the saga of the 'V2' was continued in a further and unexpected way. In the late spring of that year, certain defects on the 'Merchant Navy' engines of the Southern led to the temporary withdrawal of the whole class. Fortunately, this trouble was detected and rectified before the full summer service began, but even so for a time there would have been a numerous shortage of engines. With the building of large numbers of the new Peppercorn Pacifics, the Eastern Region had plenty of engines at that time of year and was able to lend the Southern a number of 'V2s'. These put in good work on a variety of services. I saw them at various times working the Bournemouth Belle and also sections of the West of England trains both east and west of Salisbury. Unfortunately I had no opportunity of travelling in a train hauled by one of them.

It was not necessary for an experienced locomotive engineer to study technical papers for dimensional details to appreciate that the Gresley three-cylinder designs, 4-6-2, 2-6-2, 4-6-0, 2-6-0 and 2-6-2 tank alike, had been built with greater clearances in the working parts than were then customary in British practice. An acute observer at the lineside could tell from the musical 'ring' of the motion parts when steam was shut off, quite apart from the 'clank-

The 10 am exodus from Edinburgh Waverley in 1951: on the left is 'A4' No 60011 *Empire of India* on the Aberdeen express, while seen head-on is 'A3' No 60054 *Prince of Wales* on the 10 am for Glasgow (*E.D. Bruton*)

Contrasting 'A3s' at Haymarket shed in July 1954: on the left, a standard engine, No 60099 *Call Boy*, and on the right *Humorist*, fated to be modified yet again with a twin-orifice blastpipe, double chimney and smoke deflector plates. (*E.D. Bruton*)

ing' of the connecting and coupling rods, that there was something typically 'Gresley' about the way of their going. That there was no inherent weakness in this was shown by the splendid record of reliability of the Gresley stud as a whole during the 20 years, 1921-1941, that they had been in service under his personal surveillance. The often-publicized failure of Pacific engines with overheated middle big-ends arose mainly in cases of very high power output at maximum speed. To K.J. Cook, however, with a lifetime's service on the Great Western and the exacting experience of serving as Locomotive Works Manager at Swindon under that perfectionist of Chief Mechanical Engineers, C.B. Collett, any rattles in the motion of a steam locomotive, however musically they might ring, were anathema, and he sought to eliminate them, at any rate so far as the Gresley Pacifics were concerned.

At Doncaster, manufacturing facilities in the erecting shop where the largest and most powerful engines were built were then such that the frame alignment was not so exact as the standard at Swindon, or even that at Crewe, and consequently greater clearance had to be allowed in the working parts. When he first went there, Cook was said to have remarked concerning clearances in motion parts that Swindon scrapped at the point Doncaster fitted as new! He was an expert in such matters, for in the early 1930s, when he was still Assistant to Hannington, Collett had installed the Zeiss optical system for the lining up of frames, cylinder centre-lines and main bearings. It was applied to a new batch of 'Castles' then about to be laid down, and its success was manifested in the improved performance of the engines, not necessarily in power output but in reduced maintenance costs. Cook naturally thought of this system for improving the performance of the Gresley Pacifics, but the apparatus at Swindon was of German make and was no longer available after the war. Fortunately, a British manufacturer was found who could work to the stringent specification that Cook laid down, and, from the time of the installation of the new equipment, all 'A3' and 'A4' Pacifics submitted for major overhaul at Doncaster were subjected to optical lining up of frames,.cylinders and main axle bearings.

The results were astonishing, not only acoustically but in the general working of the engines. The first one that I had personal experience of was an 'A3', in particularly enlightening circumstances. I was riding from Leeds to Edinburgh by the Midland route on the now long-defunct Thames-Forth Express, and on arrival from the south I was disappointed to find that Whitehall Junction shed had nothing better than a scruffy old 'Black Five' to take us forward to Carlisle, and, with a load of more than 300 tons, we had to be piloted. A superannuated Midland 7 ft Class '2' 4-4-0 was coupled ahead of us, and in stormy autumnal weather we had a tempestuous ride through the mountains. There was no difficulty in keeping time with two engines, but on arrival in Carlisle we found an 'A3' in absolutely spanking condition waiting to take us on to Edinburgh. Purely for the sake of creature comfort I was glad enough to exchange the somewhat spartan conditions of a run-down 'Black Five' cab for the padded bucket seat comfort of a Gresley Pacific, but when we started I could not believe my own senses. Gone completely were the clanking and vibration from the motion. We rode the sharply curving length from the junction with the Caledonian line past the former North British engine sheds in almost complete silence, and so smoothly! When we got on to the open road and could make some reason-

A Leeds and Bradford express passing Hadley Wood hauled by double-chimneyed 'A3' 4-6-2 No 60059 *Tracery*. (*Derek Cross*)

The afternoon Scotch Goods in July 1960 near Brookmans Park, hauled by 'A4' No 60017 *Silver Fox*. (*Derek Cross*)

The up Elizabethan on Ganwick curve, north of Hadley Wood, hauled by 'A4' No 60009 *Union of South Africa*. (*Derek Cross*)

able express speed, our going was immaculate—there was no other word for it. The Waverley Route, however, with its many restrictions and booked running times requiring no higher speeds than about 65 mph, was not the place to try the running qualities of these rebuilt engines, and I looked forward to riding them between Kings Cross and Newcastle.

The first opportunity that arose was soon after the Elizabethan had been put on. I was given a footplate pass for the southbound run, but although the work was absolutely top class throughout, it was one of those occasions when one could not judge the power that was being developed. A strong westerly wind was blowing throughout the length of England, and on the open stretches of line—and that meant most of the way between Berwick-on-Tweed

The Elizabethan climbing Holloway bank, with 'A4' 4-6-2 No 60028 *Walter K. Whigham*. (*B.E. Morrison*)

and Hitchin—I estimated from the engine working that our 415-ton train was pulling something like 500 tons on a calm day. The two pairs of enginemen did remarkably well to bring the train into Kings Cross 2½ minutes early on the newly accelerated schedule of 6 hrs 45 min after checks that cost 10½ minutes. The net time of 392 minutes was thus equal to an average of 60 mph overall, but the most interesting impression of this long run on *Silver Fox* was the complete absence of the usual clatter from the running gear, especially when coasting, and the evenness of the beat. Because of the strength of the wind, we did not exceed 78 mph between Alne and Beningbrough though working on 20 per cent cut-off and full regulator, nor more than 88 mph down the bank from Stoke Tunnel towards Peterborough.

A year later, the schedule of the 'non-stop' was still further quickened to 6½ hours and it became one of the hardest and most spectacular tasks ever set to a British steam locomotive. This qualification must not be misunderstood. There were other duties that

The Elizabethan crossing Selby Swing Bridge hauled by 'A4' 4-6-2 No 60017 *Silver Fox*. (*Leslie Overend*)

involved greater outputs of power for shorter distances, but in running the Elizabethan it was the length of run to be made non-stop that overrode every other consideration. There were times when the most careful management of the fire was needed to keep a good head of steam. On my first run with the accelerated train in 1954, on only the second day it ran, all went very smoothly, and I was able to see from the footplate how easily speeds approaching 100 mph were attained by these engines in the ordinary course of running. Because of certain track improvement works then under construction at Potters Bar and south thereof, the schedule inwards from Hatfield had necessarily to include some substantial recovery time, and the allowance for the 375 miles from Edinburgh to Hatfield was no more than 362 minutes. On the run south we experienced five out-of-course slowings, and still passed Hatfield 2¼ minutes early. The engine was No 60030 *Golden Fleece*, and the standard 11-coach train totalled a load of 425 tons gross behind the tender.

It is of interest to analyse the sections totalling 298.6 miles over which fast running was sustained in between the various temporary and permanent speed restrictions, and from the following table it will be seen that this length was covered at an average speed of 67.4 mph:

Analysis of high-speed running

Dist (miles)	Stretch	Actual time (min sec)		Average speed (mph)
17.4	Monktonhall Junction — East Linton	16	49	62.3
27.2	Dunbar — Marshall Meadows	26	36	61.3
47.2	Tweedmouth — Pegswood	40	45	69.5
12.2	Stannington — Heaton	11	56	61.4
64.5	Relly Mill Junction — Skelton	51	38	73.8
42.4	Templehurst — Crow Park	39	29	64.4
35.3	Newark — Tallington	31	10	68.0
7.6	Fletton Junction — Conington South	7	11	63.5
45.8	Abbots Ripton — Hatfield	40	24	68.3
298.6	Totals	265	58	67.4

The complete run of 392.7 miles from Waverley to Kings Cross occupied 385 min 10 sec, and the net time was 369 minutes, an average of 63.9 mph.

The fastest speeds were over the 42.5 miles from Darlington to Skelton Box, averaging 78.5 mph with a maximum of 84 mph, and from Corby Glen to Tallington, 12.3 miles averaging 89 mph with a maximum of 96 mph. The footplate conditions in which the latter maximum was attained are worth recalling. At Grantham the train was running just over 3 minutes early, and speed was allowed to fall to 53 mph at Stoke summit. Then the driver let the engine make its own pace, continuing to work at 15 per cent cut-off. We topped the 90 mph mark just before Little Bytham, and ran between 90 and 96 mph for about 9 miles until speed had to be reduced for a permanent way restriction south of Tallington. I was on the footplate during this fast spell and found the smoothness and quietness of the engine most impressive. The fastest overall time I have been able to trace with the Elizabethan was made in 1960 when my friend Baron Gerard Vuillet of Paris made a round trip on the footplate of engine No 60027 *Merlin*, and on the southbound run he logged an actual overall time of 380 minutes, thus arriving at Kings Cross *10 minutes early*! The net time, allowing for incidental delays, was no more than 362 minutes. *Merlin* was a favourite engine in Scotland; she carried a plaque presented by the Naval Establishment in Fife, HMS *Merlin*, past which the engine worked during one of the regular assignments of the top link Pacifics at Haymarket shed.

It was also in 1954 that I logged the first run to include a maximum of over 100 mph that I had witnessed from the footplate. It was on the up Tees-Tyne Pullman, and we had been stopped by signal at York so there was time to be made up. The engine, No 60029 *Woodcock*, was in first-class trim and the driver was going rather harder than usual from Newark onwards, using 20 per cent cut-off up to Stoke summit. Grantham was passed at 75 mph and the speed fell to 65½ mph at the top of the 1 in 200 gradient. At

The southbound Elizabethan near Brookmans Park, hauled by the Scottish-based 'A4' No 60027 *Merlin*, carrying the commorative plaques from HMS *Merlin*. (*Derek Cross*)

a point about a mile over the crest, when the speed had reached 75 mph again, the cut-off was shortened to 15 per cent, still with an almost full regulator, and the milepost timings from 97 southwards were as follows:

Milepost	Time from passing post 100 (min sec)		Average speed (mph)
97	2	18	—
96	2	58½	88.9
95	3	37½	92.3
94	4	15½	94.8
93	4	52½	97.5
92	5	28½	100.0
91	6	07½	102.7
90	6	40	98.7
89	7	17½	96.0

The regulator was eased at milepost 91 to give a much reduced steam-chest pressure of 140 lbs per sq in instead of the 220 used on the earlier part of the descent. Otherwise, I think we would have attained a much higher maximum than the actual 103½ mph, but it was, in any case, an exhilarating experience.

By the year 1958, the 'A3s' that had been fitted with the Kylchap exhaust arrangement in addition to having had their frames and cylinders optically lined up were being used turn and turn about with the 'A4s' on the principal East Coast expresses, excepting only the non-stop Scotsman in the summer months. By that time the English Electric Type 4 diesels were coming into use and it really did seem that the end of the road was approaching for

steam. In early December of that year, when I was travelling from Edinburgh to Kings Cross by the Flying Scotsman, we were hauled by steam throughout, and moreover by 'A3s'. At that time, the famous train was running non-stop from Newcastle and carrying no more than a moderate load of 11 coaches. The schedule was fast, however, and I had a footplate pass for the section south of Newcastle; on engine No 60061 *Pretty Polly* I recorded some absolutely first-class work. Signal delays from Hatfield inwards precluded a punctual arrival in London, but we were 5 minutes early when passing Sandy, 224.2 miles in 228¼ minutes, despite two severe restrictions for track relaying at Alne and before Newark. The overall time for the 268.3 miles from Newcastle to Kings Cross was 289¾ minutes, but although we were thus nearly 4 minutes late in arriving, the net time was no more than 267 minutes, an average of just over 60 mph throughout.

The engine working was immaculate. The general position of the reverser was at 15 to 20 per cent cut-off, often with the regulator only partly open. On the racing stretch of the North Eastern line we averaged 75 mph over the 32.9 miles from Darlington to Alne, and reached a maximum of 84 mph on level track with cut-off at 17 per cent, while on the flying descent from Stoke tunnel, during which a top speed of 90 mph was attained, the cut-off was 16 per cent. The regulator was not fully open and the steam-chest pressure gauge registered around 180 lbs per sq in against a boiler pressure near to the full 220 without blowing off. As with all Gresley Pacifics which had been given the 'Cook treatment' at Doncaster, *Pretty Polly*'s riding and mechanical action were faultless. It was the last time I rode on one of these engines on a high-speed

The up Tees-Tyne Pullman going dead slow over bridge construction works at Potters Bar, behind 'A4' No 60029 *Woodcock* with the author on the footplate. (*M.W. Earley*)

177

East Coast main-line express, and I could not have wished for a better finale.

The 'A4s' were being withdrawn from service from 1963 onwards, not from any inability to run but to make way for the exceedingly puissant 'Deltics'. The historic *Mallard* was earmarked for preservation, but in the last year of her active service as an ordinary traffic department engine she made a run that in many ways surpassed her high-speed achievement of July 1938. This was no well-organised publicity venture—nothing more, in fact, than a determined effort by a keen crew to make a punctual run in the face of severe delays. On the day in question, *Mallard* was on the 2 pm express from Kings Cross non-stop to Grantham on a schedule equal to the fastest ordinary East Coast expresses of pre-war days, 111 minutes for the 105.5 miles. Before leaving Kings Cross, it was known on the footplate that two severe engineering slacks would be experienced, both in locations where speed would be high, but what was not expected was a signal stop for 2½ minutes at Langley Junction, costing at least 4½ minutes in running time between Hatfield and Hitchin. Despite this and the effect of the

BR: 2 pm Kings Cross-Grantham

Engine: 'A4' 4-6-2 No 60022 *Mallard*

Load: 11 coaches, 390 tons tare, 415 tons full

Dist (miles)		Schedule (min)	Actual (min sec)		Speeds (mph)
0.0	KINGS CROSS	0	0	00	—
2.5	Finsbury Park		7	19	—
5.0	Wood Green		10	24	55
12.7	Potters Bar	18	18	38	58
17.7	HATFIELD	23	23	04	73
26.7	Langley Junction		32	20	signal stop
			34	45	
31.9	HITCHIN	37	41	34	75
37.0	Arlesey		45	19	86/83
41.1	Biggleswade		48	12	87
44.1	Sandy	46	50	18	84/87
51.7	St Neots		55	42	82
			pws		18
58.9	HUNTINGDON	60	66	29	59
62.0	Milepost 62		69	24	66
67.4	Conington South		73	34	84
			sigs		
76.4	PETERBOROUGH	80	83	00	20
			pws		20
84.8	Tallington		94	11	69
88.6	Essendine	94	97	16	78
92.2	Little Bytham		99	58	82
96.0	Milepost 96		102	45	80
97.1	Corby Glen		103	34	82
100.1	Stoke box	105	105	51	78
102.0	Great Ponton		107	18	83
105.5	GRANTHAM	111	110	39	—

slack to 18 mph before Huntingdon, the train was only 3 minutes late passing Peterborough. By that time, there were only 28 minutes left to make a punctual arrival in Grantham 29.1 miles away, much of it 'against the collar' and with the second of the two severe permanent way checks still to come.

What happened may be studied in detail from the accompanying tabulated log. Suffice to say that the uphill running from the 20 mph slow was the most astonishing piece of power output I have seen from a Gresley Pacific. I was not travelling in the train myself, but the timing was done by one of the correspondents who wrote regularly to me during my authorship of the 'Locomotive Practice and Performance' feature in *The Railway Magazine* which I contributed monthly from 1959 until December 1980. Between Peterborough and Stoke summit my friend made a continuous record at every milepost, and, as the log shows, the 11.5 uphill miles from Essendine were covered in 8 min 35 sec at an average of 80.6 mph, while the sustained minimum speed on the 1 in 200 up to milepost 96 was 80 mph. This tremendous effort, which involved an output of 2,450 equivalent drawbar horsepower, may well be set as a record for all time, and it brought the train into Grantham on time.

13

The Pacifics—deployment and preservation

One of the results of the changes in the Regional boundaries of British Railways around 1960 was that the North Eastern Region extended almost to Skipton, and that the former Leeds running sheds of Farnley and Whitehall Junction came within the jurisdiction of my good friend F.H. Petty, Motive Power Superintendent, North Eastern Region. With many new diesels allocated to the East Coast Main Line, some of the 'A3' Pacifics became redundant and Petty transferred some of them to Leeds for use on the double-home turns to Glasgow via the Midland and G&SW route. After the Leeds men had taken the measure of what were obviously strange machines to drivers and firemen who had grown up on Midland compounds and the Stanier types of 4-6-0, they were voted the best ever. But before coming to an account of the work they did over the strenuous conditions of the Settle and Carlisle line it is important to record in this account of the locomotives of Sir Nigel Gresley another memorable run by one of the most famous of them all, *Papyrus*. Then carrying her BR number 60097, she was one of the select band of Gresley Pacifics attached to the Haymarket top link, two crews being allocated to each engine. The performance of the link as a whole, in its timekeeping, its economy, and its freedom from failure must surely have been second to none among enginemen and locomotives continuously engaged in heavy and fast duties.

In connection with some other work on the North-east coast I was given a footplate pass for the down Flying Scotsman from Newcastle to Edinburgh, and although no prior arrangements had been made on this particular afternoon, not even the presence of a locomotive inspector, I was delighted to find *Papyrus* on the job. Her driver was one of the three brothers Smith, all in the Haymarket top link, backed up by a perfect artist of a fireman in Angus Wylie. In these days when steam working is outmoded one sometimes hears remarks about the indignity of men 'having to shovel coal for a living'. If it were nothing more than coal heaving I would agree; but to watch a fireman like Wylie at work, anticipating his driver's needs, never wasting a pound of coal or steam, suiting his control of the boiler feed and the actual firing to the fluctuations in demand of the road and the schedule, and withall keeping the footplate—and himself!—clean, was a complete abnegation of the idea of indignity. The traditions of steam on the footplate die hard, and I know of many engineers, trained on locomotives, and who have subsequently obtained positions of great distinction in their profession, who rarely miss the chance of a glimpse of 'auld lang syne' on the footplate.

The accompanying table shows the exploits of *Papyrus* that spring afternoon, when Ralph Smith and Angus Wylie gave such an immaculate display. They left Newcastle on time, with 142 minutes in which to read Edinburgh. This was not an unduly hard task, even with a load of 510 tons, but through some conflicting local traffic movement we were stopped at Heaton and lost 4 minutes at the very outset. After that there was a steady recovery of time and we eventually arrived in Edinburgh 2 minutes early. The engine was run with the regulator full open, for all the hard and fast work. The boiler pressure was kept around 205 to 215 lbs per sq in and the cut-off varied from the usual 15 per cent for

BR, NE & Scottish Regions: Flying Scotsman, Newcastle-Edinburgh

Engine: Class 'A3' 4-6-2 No 60098 *Papyrus*
Load: 477 tons tare, 510 tons full

Dist (miles)		Actual (min sec)		Speeds (mph)
0.0	NEWCASTLE	0	00	—
—		sig stop		
1.7	Heaton	6	50	—
5.0	Forest Hall	12	51	39
9.9	Cramlington	18	31	58/54½
13.9	Stannington	22	21	70
16.6	MORPETH	25	15	slack
20.2	Longhirst	29	30	66
—		pws		40
28.5	Acklington	38	49	69
34.8	ALNMOUTH	44	42	65
39.4	Little Mill	50	01	48½
46.0	Chathill	56	05	75
51.6	Belford	61	02	63½
58.6	Beal	66	53	76
63.5	Scremerston	71	18	55/60
65.7	Tweedmouth Junction	73	50	50
66.9	BERWICK	75	24	—
72.5	Burnmouth	—		62½
78.2	Reston Junction	88	58	57½
83.2	Grantshouse	94	58	49
87.9	Cocksburnspath	99	40	72/59
95.2	DUNBAR	106	25	62½
100.9	East Linton	112	13	60
106.6	DREM JUNCTION	117	32	69/61½
114.9	Prestonpans	125	10	67
118.3	Monktonhall Junction	128	39	—
121.4	Portobello	133	35	
—		sigs		
124.4	EDINBURGH	139	48	—

Net time: 134 minutes

all the fast running south of the Border, to 20-25 per cent along the Lothian coast, where the gradients, though undulating, are in the aggregate slightly adverse between Dunbar and Preston-pans. One could not take advantage of the favourable stretch onwards to Portobello, because of slight civil engineering restrictions.

Some of the most impressive work, from the viewpoint of loco-motive power output, followed the crossing of the Royal Border Bridge, and on the ascent to Grantshouse summit, in the Lammer-moor hills. The ascent is at first 1 in 190, and Smith gave the engine 37 per cent cut-off immediately we were through Berwick. Wylie had for several minutes been building up in readiness for this, and despite the heavy demands for steam, with the engine gradu-ally accelerating this 510-ton train to 46 mph on the gradient, the boiler pressure showed a tendency to rise, while the water level remained quite steady. The one break in the climbing took us rapidly up to 62½ mph near Ayton, and on the continuous 1 in 200 gradient from Reston Junction to the summit we settled down to a steady 49 to 50 mph. This stretch of line includes much cur-vature, with our long train undoubtedly caused some variation in the rolling resistance of the stock. Cut-off was gradually in-creased from 20 per cent at Reston to 32 at the summit. In other circumstances this might be considered a large increase, but in the last miles Wylie was easing the firing a little to avoid blowing off when steam would be shut off completely for the descent of Cockburnspath bank. We thus topped Grantshouse summit with only 195 lbs per sq in 'on the clock', and the driver was having to use a longer cut-off to maintain speed.

After some of the 'A3s' previously at Gateshead had been trans-ferred to Whitehall Junction, Mr Petty gave me a footplate pass to ride the down Thames-Clyde Express non-stop from Leeds to Carlisle. The maximum tare load for one of these engines had been fixed at 405 tons, the same as that for the 'Converted Scot' 4-6-0s. The schedule in August 1960 had not been accelerated to the fastest times worked between the two World Wars, and was, in fact, 1 minute slower than the timing of the 4.7 pm from Leeds when the first post-grouping dynamometer car trials were run in December 1923, 136 minutes for the 112.8 miles. This schedule provided for very easy running down from Aisgill summit to Carlisle, with 50 minutes allowed for the 48½ miles. On my first trip we had almost a maximum load, 11 coaches, 390 tons tare, 410 tons full, with engine No 60077 *The White Knight*. In former days, as engine No 2576, she was fitted with the ACFI feed-water heater, when the original 180 lb boiler was fitted, but in 1960 she was a standard 'A3'. We had a flourishing send-off from Leeds, with the late Bishop Eric Treacy to photograph us, and a start less than 2 minutes late; but after some final initial running we were

in deep trouble on the Settle and Carlisle line.

Eventually we arrived at Carlisle 13½ minutes late and had to change to another engine for the continuation run to Glasgow. Mr Petty at once offered me another trip but I could not go until mid-October and then the train was down to its minimum winter formation, only nine coaches.

To see the speed at which Gresley Pacifics could really run over this superb road I had to wait another two years when my wife and I were invited as guests of the West Riding Branch of the Railway Correspondence and Travel Society, me to lecture to a gather-

'A3s' on the Midland: No 60077 *The White Knight* climbs to Aisgill summit with the up Thames-Clyde Express.

The up Thames-Clyde Express between Rise Hill tunnel and Dent hauled by 'A3' 4-6-2 No 60082 *Neil Gow. (both Bishop Eric Treacy)*

ing of their members in Leeds, and to join them next day on a 'Three Summits Tour' from Leeds, including Aisgill, Beattock and Shap. On the first stage of the tour a Gresley 'A4' was to be used from Leeds to Carlisle, and after the Scottish part the same engine would be working us back from Carlisle over Shap and then down the Ingleton line to the 'Little North Western' at the moorland Clapham Junction, and so to Settle Junction and back on to the Midland main line. At the meeting in Leeds on the Saturday evening it was announced that the Gresley 'A4' to be used was No 60023 *Golden Eagle*.

On the following morning the train arrived at Skipton with the left hand injector failed. Steam was being hurriedly raised on a 'Black Five' that was on the shed at Skipton, but everyone hoped that such a resort as double-heading the 'A4' or, even worse, taking her off altogether, would be avoided. With repairs completed, to everyone's relief the injector picked up, and some 45 minutes after the advertised time was started. But we were not doing well on the 'Long Drag' and after Horton a 'thumbs down' signal from the footplate indicated that they were in trouble again. Actually that injector had failed again before Hellifield and the whole journey to Carlisle was performed with only one injector in action.

Downhill from Aisgill, at first we ran some considerable distance without steam; but the right-hand injector was working satisfactorily, and after Kirkby Stephen, with the water rising in the gauges, the regulator was open again. An 'A4' needs little encouragement to 'fly', especially on so favourable a road, and from Crosby *Golden Eagle* certainly spread her wings. I would not be so dogmatic as to assert that Sunday 30 June 1963 witnessed the absolute record for the Aisgill-Carlisle descent; but certainly the time of 31 min 17 sec for the 40.9 miles from Mallerstang box to Cumwhinton, with its average speed of 78.4 mph, was the fastest that had ever been published in *The Railway Magazine* up to that time. Still faster times might have been achieved had it not been for the restriction to 70 mph imposed over the summit north of Armathwaite. Nevertheless, to run a 360-ton load from Hellifield to Carlisle in 82½ min with an ailing engine was an excellent achievement. The time might have been 1¼ min less but for the signal check at the finish, and we said *au revoir* to *Golden Eagle* and her crew with Inspector Pullan's remark that he would have her right by evening or 'die in the attempt'.

After our circular tour in Scotland we came back to *Golden Eagle* waiting for the final leg of the journey, and this time the crew were all smiles, but once again bad luck dogged our progress. Delays on the G&SW line had made the train so much out of its advertised path that from Carlisle the Keswick diesel was despatched ahead of us. When *Golden Eagle* and her crew began to develop some truly magnificent hill-climbing, in ample amends for the dis-

appointment of the Settle Junction-Blea Moor climb earlier in the day, I feared that sooner or later we must be involved in signal checks. Nevertheless our progress as far south as Plumpton was brilliant. The log is shown herewith in very full detail and to appreciate the merit of the speeds it is only necessary to refer to the gradients. To Wreay the ascent is continuous at 1 in 131. Then, between that point and milepost 58, the inclination varies between 1 in 184-228-172 and lastly a mile at 1 in 114. Here the speeds were

'A4s' on the Caledonian line: engine No 60011 *Empire of India* on the up Bon Accord Aberdeen to Glasgow express at Bridge of Allan. (*Derek Cross*)

London Midland Region: Carlisle-Hellifield (via Shap), RCTS Special, 30 June 1963

Engine: Class 'A4' 4-6-2 No 60023 *Golden Eagle*
Load: 10 coaches, 329 tons tare, 360 tons full

Dist (miles)		Schedule (min)	Actual (min sec)		Speeds (mph)
0.0	CARLISLE	0	0	00	—
1.4	Carlisle No 13 box		4	18	—
3.1	Milepost 66		7	24	37½
4.9	Wreay		10	04	45
6.1	Milepost 63		11	29	51
7.4	Southwaite		12	53	54
9.1	Milepost 60		14	41	59
10.1	Milepost 59		15	42	58
12.1	Milepost 57		17	45	58½
13.1	Plumpton	23	18	42	66
16.1	Milepost 53		20	32	68 (max)
			sig stop		—
17.9	PENRITH	30	30	22	—
19.1	Milepost 50		32	39	54½
21.1	Milepost 48		34	02	53½
23.1	Milepost 46		37	18	53
25.1	Milepost 44		39	34	53
27.1	Milepost 42		41	49	54½
29.4	Shap		44	15	61/57
31.4	Shap Summit	55	46	19	60
33.9	Scout Green		48	25	82½
36.9	TEBAY	61	51	45	—

held between the narrow limits of 57 and 59 mph. Plumpton sees the first real break in the climbing, with nearly 2 miles of dead level, and here speed rose to 68 mph; but it was just beyond this point, when there was a chance of getting into the seventies through Penrith and taking a real 'bash' at Shap, that adverse signals were first sighted. Eventually we were stopped for 3 min outside Penrith, while the diesel was at the platform.

We were lucky to get no more than the one check; but its effect was to cost us at least 9½ min in running. Once clear of Penrith, however, some grand work was done up to Shap. We touched 54½ mph at Eden Valley Junction, then settled down to a steady and unvarying 53 mph, and the full 7 miles of continuous 1 in 125 ascent between mileposts 49 and 42 were covered in 7 min 54 sec at an average speed of 53.2 mph. This was the biggest power output of the day, and represented an equivalent drawbar horsepower of about 1,710. We touched 61 mph on the brief level past Shap station; took the last 1¼ miles at 1 in 106-130 without falling below 57 mph; and passed the summit box at exactly 60 mph. We began the descent briskly, with a maximum speed of 82½ mph, but unfortunately we had to stop at Tebay to put down one pilotman and pick up another, and because of this the speed descending the bank had to be checked before there was a chance of getting another really high maximum out of *Golden Eagle*. I have not tabulated the rest of the run to Hellifield; while of interest to me personally in view of my schooltime association with the district it involved little if anything beyond down-hill running.

The 'Three Summits Tour' of 1963 did not mark the ending of the long reign of the Gresley Pacifics as regular traffic department locomotives, although the end was not then far away. Worse than this, from the end of 1968 British Railways, with one notable exception, forbade the running of any of the privately preserved steam locomotives anywhere on the system. The exception was the 'A3' Pacific *Flying Scotsman*, at that time owned by Alan Pegler, formerly a member of the Eastern Region Area Board. It was through Pegler's enterprise that the exciting project of celebrating the fiftieth anniversary of running the Flying Scotsman train non-stop between Kings Cross and Edinburgh by re-enacting the trip. Non-stop running on the summer service had been discontinued since the 'Deltics' took over in 1962. While the engine was in excellent condition, and the relatively moderate load scheduled for the train was not expected to make any inordinate demands for steam and coal consumption, with water supply it was another matter. Only three sets of water troughs remained in commission, those at Scrooby (near Bawtry), Wiske Moor (north of Northallerton), and at Lucker, Northumberland, and to provide against the deficiency from the normal thus involved, Pegler had purchased a second tender, providing an extra 6,000 gallons of water.

What was not anticipated, however, was that the water troughs were not full, and at the very first less than 1,000 gallons were scooped. The next hazard was a broken rail north of Doncaster, which involved almost a dead stop. The whole journey provided an almost continuous succession of alarming incidents, alarming to the chances of getting through to Edinburgh non-stop, but as I told in *The Railway Magazine* of July 1968 we did it, arriving in 464 min 57 sec for the 392.7 miles, only 5 minutes late after delays amounting to some 28 minutes *en route*, a net average speed of 54 mph. The load was one of 7 coaches behind the second tender, 250 tons tare. The second tender was also carried when in the following year Pegler took the engine for the very ambitious tour of North American railways, during which an immense amount of public and railway interest was aroused. The engine and its two tenders sailed from Brocklebank East Dock, Liverpool, on 19 September 1969 and, after a long and eventful saga on American and Canadian railways lasting more than two years, at one time it seemed she would never return.

The 'crunch' developed in the early summer of 1972 after 'Flying Scotsman Enterprises' had embarked on the venturesome project of running the train along the San Francisco Belt Railroad, carrying fare-paying passengers. The project, and the preliminary negotiations, were described in an article in *The Railway Magazine* for August 1972 by George Hinchcliffe, the intrepid General Manager of 'Flying Scotsman Enterprises'. Unfortunately interest, both from business and enthusiasts, proved to be lacking, and financial difficulties became such that not only was the service withdrawn and the locomotive and rolling-stock removed for storage at Sharpe Army Base, but also Alan Pegler himself had to face a London bankruptcy hearing in October of the same year.

Flying Scotsman on an unfrequented line in south-west Scotland, with a Gainsborough Model Railway Society special near Shieldhill on the Dumfries-Lockerbie branch in 1965. (*Derek Cross*)

187

Flying Scotsman, with second tender, on tour in North America, in the Canadian National roundhouse at Toronto in 1970.

Flying Scotsman on the Cumbrian Coast Express at Ravenglass. (*Derek Cross*)

Worse than this, the various creditors, among which were three leading American railroads, were pressing for repayment, and in the USA a somewhat jaundiced view was taken of the rescue operation being mounted in the City of London. Fortunately one of those taking a leading part in this was the Hon W.H. McAlpine, and he asked George Hinchcliffe to go back to the USA to check up on the situation. It was not a moment too premature, for as he told in an article in *The Railway Magazine* in August 1973 entitled 'Return of the Prodigal', at the very time he arrived in Washington the three principal railroad creditors were seeking a court order to seize the train and sell it. How the train was rescued and brought back to England is told vividly in that article.

I had the pleasure of meeting George Hinchcliffe many years before the transatlantic visit of *Flying Scotsman* when he was still a village schoolmaster at Stourton-by-Stow, in Lincolnshire, and a mechanical engineering pillar of the Gainsborough Model Railway Club. Already he had been associated with some of Alan Pegler's railway excursions. But I knew him best in after years when he was the boss at Steamtown, Carnforth, and I had the privilege of riding *Flying Scotsman* on the Cumbrian Coast Express through to Ravenglass. But I must retrace my steps to the year 1967, before the 'official' end of steam on British Railways, when the preserved locomotives were still permitted to run at the maximum line speeds. The 'A4' Locomotive Society, which now owns and runs the historic engine No 4498 *Sir Nigel Gresley*, made an inaugural run on 1 April 1967, with the engine repainted in garter blue and bearing the original number, from Crewe to Carlisle and back, and did some excellent running with a 450-ton train, much to the delight of the numerous enthusiasts travelling. But the climax of Gresley Pacific performance was surely reached on 28 October 1967 with The Border Limited, again from Crewe to Carlisle. I was not a passenger myself on this occasion, but I was furnished with a very complete log by Mr H.G. Ellison.

In *The Railway Magazine* for February 1968 I wrote that the train went out of Crewe in a style enough to make some of the Liverpool electrics look to their laurels, for in just over 10 minutes from the dead start *Sir Nigel Gresley*, with his load of 385 tons, was travelling at 96 mph! Once out from 'under the wires', however, the pace had to be moderated to suit the reduced speed limit of the non-electrified line. Even so, to reach Warrington, 24 miles, in 22 min 40 sec was a most exhilarating start. On the ensuing section from Warrington to Preston, the train was beset by checks, and so took 40 min 5 sec for this distance of 27 miles. Then they set out on the non-stop run to Carlisle, for which the ultra-cautious time of 118 minutes had been laid down to a working stop at Carlisle No 13 box, 88.6 miles.

The immediate start out of Preston can never be very brisk, and

Sir Nigel Gresley as first restored to garter blue livery and with the original number 4498, climbing Shap with an 'A4' Locomotive Society special in April 1967. (*Derek Cross*)

Later on the same day, engine No 4498 on the turntable at Kingmoor sheds, Carlisle. (*Derek Cross*)

the engine was taken gently over the labyrinth of crossings until the Blackpool lines had veered away to the left. Then the acceleration was to some purpose, and the speed soared to 84 mph on the level at Garstang. Then came two permanent way checks, one at Scorton intermediate signals, and the second at Lancaster No 1 Junction. The two altogether cost about 8½ minutes in running and the engine was not pressed to a very rapid acceleration from Lancaster; the speed rose only from 61 to 64 mph along the level between Hest Bank and Carnforth. But after passing the latter station the engine was magnificently opened out to make an average speed of all but 63 mph right up to Shap Summit. From the accompanying log it will be seen that the sharp rise to milepost

9½ was cleared at 59 mph and then the speed rose to all but 80 mph on the level before tackling Grayrigg bank. The time of 12 min 7 sec for the 12.6 miles from Milnthorpe to Grayrigg must be something of a record with a gross load of 385 tons, although of course the climbing on the upper part of the bank does not match the classic effort of the LMS Stanier 4-6-2 No 6244 *King George VI* with the wartime 10.05 from Euston, when, with a 475-ton train, the speed was 59 mph sustained at Lambrigg and 57 mph over the summit. Nevertheless, this performance of 4498 was a grand effort, and judging from the brilliant acceleration that followed from Low Gill, was in no way beyond the continuous steaming capacity of the boiler.

Then came Shap itself with a phenomenal ascent, and an average speed over the 4 miles of 1 in 75 ascent between mileposts 33½ and 37½ of 54½ mph. Making careful allowance for the loss of kinetic energy of engine and train by the deceleration dur-

The Border Limited, 28 October 1967

Engine: Class 'A4' No 4498 *Sir Nigel Gresley*
Load: 351 tons tare, 385 tons full

Dist (miles)		Schedule (min)	Actual (min sec)	Speeds (mph)
0.0	PRESTON	0	0 00	—
4.7	Barton		8 13	65
7.4	Brock		10 29	78
9.5	Garstang	12	12 00	84
			pws	—
12.7	Scorton		16 07	15*
18.0	Onbeck		22 00	70
			pws	—
19.9	Lancaster No 1 box		27 15	20*
21.0	LANCASTER	24	28 52	52
27.3	Carnforth	31	35 16	70
30.5	Milepost 9½		38 16	59
34.5	Milnthorpe		41 37	79
36.4	Hincaster Junction (site)		43 11	71
40.1	OXENHOLME	46	46 27	63
45.2	Lambrigg Crossing		51 38	56
47.1	Grayrigg		53 44	52
48.9	Low Gill		55 30	58*
53.1	Tebay	68	59 21	73
56.1	Scout Green		62 12	54
58.7	Shap Summit	80	65 13	47
			pws	
60.9	Shap		68 38	20*
68.0	Clifton		99 22	60 (max)
72.2	PENRITH	94	83 54	50*
77.0	Plumpton	99	88 02	84
79.3	Calthwaite		89 38	88
82.7	Southwaite		92 06	78
85.2	Wreay		94 07	70*
86.8	Brisco		95 29	74
88.6	CARLISLE No 13 (home signal)	118	97 43	—

* Speed restriction

191

Sir Nigel Gresley nearing Shap Summit with The Border Limited on 28 October 1967 (*W.B. Greenfield*)

ing this period, it would appear that the average equivalent drawbar horsepower over this four miles of ascent was around 2,550. This was an exceptional piece of work in every way and one of the finest Shap ascents ever recorded with steam. The occasion was splendidly documented photographically by Mr W.B. Greenfield whose result is reproduced here. The photograph is, however, much more than a mere record of a 'train in motion'. It reveals in the clearness of the exhaust, and the slight wisp of steam from the safety valves, that the working of the engine was absolutely ideal—a wonderful piece of work in every way.

There was a permanent way slack just after Shap summit, and speed was severely restrained thereafter until Penrith had been passed. Then *Sir Nigel Gresley* was allowed to run and there was a brilliant finish, with a top speed of 88 mph near Calthwaite. The train was stopped, by order, at Carlisle No 13 home signal, but Mr Ellison estimates a net time of 86½ minutes to Citadel station.

I have prepared on page 191 a somewhat abridged version of the log compiled in such detail by Mr Ellison, and published in *The Railway Magazine*, but abridged or not it gives an impressive picture of an outstanding locomotive performance, which while it was made over a 'foreign' line aptly summarises what the Gresley Pacifics could do when fully extended.

The embargo on all running by preserved steam locomotives over the entire British Railways network had been no more than partially lifted when the time came for the Centenary of the opening of the Settle and Carlisle line to be celebrated in 1976. No steam was then permitted on the line itself, and the best that could be provided for the anniversary special was steam haulage between

Carnforth and Hellifield, with the Midland compound 4-4-0 No 1000 and a Stanier 'Black Five' 4-6-0 which had prior associations with the line. But when my wife and I arrived at Giggleswick on the Friday evening it was to learn that both ex-LMS engines had failed and that an SOS had been sent to the National Railway Museum at York to borrow *Flying Scotsman*, rather than have the special hauled throughout by diesel, as would in any case be the power from Hellifield to Carlisle and back to Settle. On the Saturday morning we travelled to Carnforth and found that a little of the old-time flavour was being furnished by having the little North Western 2-4-0 *Hardwicke* to pilot *Flying Scotsman* to Hellifield.

When in June 1978 British Railways began to run its own excursions, using certain of the preserved steam locomotives, the Gresley types were very much in demand; indeed, for working the Cumbrian Coast Express between Carnforth and Sellafield, *Flying Scotsman* and *Sir Nigel Gresley* were in daily use throughout the summer. In *The Railway Magazine* of February 1979 I wrote:

'To say that the running of the Cumbrian Coast Express during last summer was an outstanding success would now be the merest platitude. It must be set down as one of the most remarkable excursion train workings of all time. By the last week but one in which it ran during 1978, when I had the privilege of an engine pass from Carnforth to Sellafield and back, one might have imagined that the novelty and interest of the train as a popular spectacle would have diminished somewhat. Not a bit of it; vantage points all along the line were thronged with enthusiastic spectators, and at a guess I would think that the number of photographs taken of us on the double journey must have been approaching the four-figure mark.

Sir Nigel Gresley on exhibition in Carlisle Citadel station in May 1970. (*Derek Cross*)

It was a moving experience for me, knowing the Furness Railway of old, and how the big names of the railway photographic world would never seem to penetrate its fastnesses beyond the yard at Carnforth!'

Of course the Gresley LNER Pacifics 4472 *Flying Scotsman* and 4498 *Sir Nigel Gresley* are a never-ceasing source of attraction, at any time, and the folks at Steamtown certainly saw to it that they took the road in truly regal splendour. On the morning of my trip I arrived at Carnforth in time to see the finishing touches being put on to their respective *toilettes*, by two young lady cleaners whose enthusiasm was boundless. Imagine getting up at the crack of dawn, driving more than 30 miles over lakeland roads—as one of them did from her home beside Ullswater—and then getting under an engine, to make sure that the rods, axles and all else between the frames was as spotless as the external paintwork.

I travelled behind *Flying Scotsman* little more than a month later on the second of the special trains run in memory of the late Bishop Eric Treacy, between Hellifield and Appleby, where he had died in the previous May. While we waited for the train from the south, No 4472 was in readiness and I met again the lady cleaner who had been so much in evidence at Carnforth before my foot-plate run on the Cumbrian Coast Express. She had ridden on the engine from Carnforth to Hellifield, with her rags at the ready, in case 'her engine' should need some touching up in its spotless toilet before taking out The Lord Bishop train. In the course of the climb from Settle Junction to Blea Moor with our heavy train of 485 tons I was several times asked how the performance of the

Mallard on an LCGB tour train, the West Countryman, at Tiverton Junction. (*Ivo Peters*)

engine compared with my previous recordings with trains of comparable weight. The average speed over the last 10 miles of ascent was 25.5 mph, and while in pre-war days I had recorded a speed of 37.1 mph over this same stretch with a 470-ton load, this was with an LNWR small-boilered 'Claughton' class 4-6-0, piloted by a Midland 7 ft Class 2 4-4-0. The comparison is not entirely fair, because it is one thing to work these preserved engines for short periods, as on the climbs to Lindal Moor with the Cumbrian Coast Express, but it would be quite another to flog them for half an hour or more ascending the 'Long Drag'.

Mallard alongside *King George V* on a most unphotographic day at Swindon. (*Peter W. Gray*)

Flying Scotsman in Australia, on 18 October 1988, at Wallongong for a crew change during the trial trip. (*J. Costigan*)

Preserved 'K4' 2-6-0 No 3442 *The Great Marquess* on an eleven-coach train on the Severn Valley Railway. (*Phil Waterfield*)

So in conclusion a word about the other preserved Gresley locomotives. Of the five remaining A4 Pacifics, *Dominion of Canada* was presented to the Canadian Railroad Historical Association for display in their museum near Montreal, and *Dwight D. Eisenhower*, formerly LNER *Golden Shuttle*, was presented by Lord Beeching for display at the National Railroad Museum of Green Bay, Wisconsin, USA. As a national relic of the first importance, *Mallard*, now restored to her original condition with the valances added, is at the National Railway Museum at York, when not on various excursions, while *Union of South Africa*, No 60009, owned by John Cameron, is on the Lochty Railway in Fife. *Bittern*, originally No 4464 of the LNER, was distinguished as the only 'A4' to be allocated to Heaton shed, and as such performed on the down Flying Scotsman between Kings Cross and Newcastle and on the 10.5 am down when the summer 'non-stop' was running. She is based now at the Dinting Railway Centre and her present owners have wrought a transformation in her appearance by renaming her *Silver Link*, with the appropriate number and original livery. Of the remaining Gresley locomotives that have been preserved, *Green Arrow*, the first of the 'V2s', is based at York and very much in demand for enthusiast specials; the 'N2' 0-6-2 tank No 4744 is in the care of the Gresley Society, while the remaining 'D49' class 4-4-0, No 246 *Morayshire*, is with the Scottish Railway Preservation Society at Falkirk.

Last among the preserved Gresley locomotives is the much cherished 'K4' 2-6-0 No 3442 *The Great Marquess*. Normally based on the Severn Valley Railway, it was recommissioned in April 1989 after an extensive overhaul which took the indefatigable volunteers at Bridgnorth eight years to complete. Fortunately it was completed in time for the owner, the late Earl of Lindsay, to be present, before his untimely death at the early age of 63 on 1 August 1989.

Appendix

List of named engines

1. Non-streamlined 'Pacifics'

1924 or later No	Name	Built at	BR No
4470	Great Northern	Doncaster	
4471	Sir Frederick Banbury	Doncaster	60102
4472	Flying Scotsman	Doncaster	60103
4473	Solario	Doncaster	60104
4474	Victor Wild	Doncaster	60105
4475	Flying Fox	Doncaster	60106
4476	Royal Lancer	Doncaster	60107
4477	Gay Crusader	Doncaster	60108
4478	Hermit	Doncaster	60109
4479	Robert the Devil	Doncaster	60110
4480	Enterprise	Doncaster	60111
4481	St Simon	Doncaster	60112
2543	Melton	Doncaster	60044
2544	Lemberg	Doncaster	60045
2545	Diamond Jubilee	Doncaster	60046
2546	Donovan	Doncaster	60047
2547	Doncaster	Doncaster	60048
2548	Galtee More	Doncaster	60049
2549	Persimmon	Doncaster	60050
2550	Blink Bonny	Doncaster	60051
2551	Prince Palatine	Doncaster	60052
2552	Sansovino	Doncaster	60053
2553	Prince of Wales[1]	Doncaster	60054
2554	Woolwinder	Doncaster	60055
2555	Centenary	Doncaster	60056
2556	Ormonde	Doncaster	60057
2557	Blair Athol	Doncaster	60058
2558	Tracery	Doncaster	60059
2559	The Tetrarch	Doncaster	60060
2560	Pretty Polly	Doncaster	60061
2561	Minoru	Doncaster	60062
2562	Isinglass	Doncaster	60063
2563	William Whitelaw[2]	North British Loco Co	60064
2564	Knight of the Thistle	North British Loco Co	60065
2565	Merry Hampton	North British Loco Co	60066
2566	Ladas	North British Loco Co	60067
2567	Sir Visto	North British Loco Co	60068

[1] No 2553 was for a short time before 1926 named Manna
[2] No 2563 was renamed Tagalie in July 1941

1924 or later No	Name	Built at	BR No
2568	Sceptre	North British Loco Co	60069
2569	Gladiateur	North British Loco Co	60070
2570	Tranquil	North British Loco Co	60071
2571	Sunstar	North British Loco Co	60072
2572	St Gatien	North British Loco Co	60073
2573	Harvester	North British Loco Co	60074
2574	St Frusquin	North British Loco Co	60075
2575	Galopin	North British Loco Co	60076
2576	The White Knight	North British Loco Co	60077
2577	Night Hawk	North British Loco Co	60078
2578	Bayardo	North British Loco Co	60079
2579	Dick Turpin	North British Loco Co	60080
2580	Shotover	North British Loco Co	60081
2581	Neil Gow	North British Loco Co	60082
2582	Sir Hugo	North British Loco Co	60083
2743	Felstead	Doncaster	60089
2744	Grand Parade	Doncaster	60090
2745	Captain Cuttle	Doncaster	60091
2746	Fairway	Doncaster	60092
2747	Coronach	Doncaster	60093
2748	Colorado	Doncaster	60094
2749	Flamingo	Doncaster	60095
2750	Papyrus	Doncaster	60096
2751	Humorist	Doncaster	60097
2752	Spion Kop	Doncaster	60098
2595	Trigo	Doncaster	60084
2596	Manna	Doncaster	60085
2597	Gainsborough	Doncaster	60086
2795	Call Boy	Doncaster	60099
2796	Spearmint	Doncaster	60100
2797	Cicero	Doncaster	60101
2598	Blenheim	Doncaster	60087
2599	Book Law	Doncaster	60088
2500	Windsor Lad	Doncaster	60035
2501	Colombo	Doncaster	60036
2502	Hyperion	Doncaster	60037
2503	Firdaussi	Doncaster	60038
2504	Sandwich	Doncaster	60039
2505	Cameronian	Doncaster	60040
2506	Salmon Trout	Doncaster	60041
2507	Singapore	Doncaster	60042
2508	Brown Jack	Doncaster	60043

2. Class 'A4' streamlined Pacifics — all built at Doncaster

Original number	Original name	Later name (if any) and date of change	BR No
2509	Silver Link		60014
2510	Quicksilver		60015
2511	Silver King		60016
2512	Silver Fox		60017
4482	Golden Eagle		60023

199

Original number	Original name	Later name (if any) and date of change	BR No
4483	Kingfisher		60024
4484	Falcon		60025
4485	Kestrel	Miles Beevor (11/47)	60026
4486	Merlin		60027
4487	Sea Eagle	Walter K. Whigham (10/47)	60028
4488	Union of South Africa		60009
4489	Woodcock	Dominion of Canada (6/37)	60010
4490	Empire of India		60011
4491	Commonwealth of Australia		60012
4492	Dominion of New Zealand		60013
4493	Woodcock		60029
4494	Osprey	Andrew K. McCosh (10/47)	60003
4495	Great Snipe	Golden Fleece (9/37)	60030
4496	Golden Shuttle	Dwight D. Eisenhower (9/45)	60008
4497	Golden Plover		60031
4498	Sir Nigel Gresley		60007
4462	Great Snipe	William Whitelaw (7/41)	60004
4463	Sparrow Hawk		60018
4464	Bittern		60019
4465	Guillemot		60020
4466	Herring Gull	Sir Ralph Wedgwood (1/44)	60006
4467	Wild Swan		60021
4468	Mallard		60022
4469	Gadwall	Sir Ralph Wedgwood (3/39)	—[3]
4499	Pochard	Sir Murrough Wilson (4/39)	60002
4500	Garganey	Sir Ronald Matthews (3/39)	60001
4900	Gannet		60032
4901	Capercaillie	Charles H. Newton (9/42) Sir Charles Newton (6/43)	60005
4902	Seagull		60033
4903	Peregrine	Lord·Faringdon (3/48)	60034

[3] Engine 4469 destroyed in an air raid at York

3. 'D49' class three-cylinder 4-4-0s
(a) 'Shire' series

Original No	Name	BR No
234	Yorkshire	62700
236	Lancashire	62707
245	Lincolnshire	62710
246	Morayshire	62712
249	Aberdeenshire	62713
250	Perthshire	62714
251	Derbyshire	62701
253	Oxfordshire	62702
256	Hertfordshire	62703
264	Stirlingshire	62704
265	Lanarkshire	62705
266	Forfarshire	62706

Original No	Name	BR No
270	Argyllshire	62708
277	Berwickshire	62709
281	Dumbartonshire	62711
306	Roxburghshire	62715
307	Kincardineshire	62716
309	Banffshire	62717
310	Kinross-shire	62718
311	Peebles-shire	62719
318	Cambridgeshire	62720
320	Warwickshire	62721
322	Huntingdonshire	62722
327	Nottinghamshire	62723
329	Inverness-shire	62725
335	Bedfordshire	62724
336[4]	Buckinghamshire	62726
352[4]	Leicestershire	62727
2753	Cheshire	62728
2754	Rutlandshire	62729
2755	Berkshire	62730
2756	Selkirkshire	62731
2757	Dumfries-shire	62732
2758	Northumberland	62733
2759	Cumberland	62734
2760	Westmorland	62235

[4] Engines 336 and 352 were built experimentally with RC poppet valve gear, and after the later 'Hunt' series was built similarly fitted, these two engines were renamed *The Meynell* and *The Quorn* respectively.

(b) The Hunt series

Original No	Name	BR No
201	The Bramham Moor	62736
211	The York and Ainstey	62737
220	The Zetland	62738
232	The Badsworth	62739
235	The Bedale	62740
247	The Blankney	62741
255	The Braes of Derwent	62742
267	The Cleveland	62743
273	The Holderness	62744
282	The Hurworth	62745
283	The Middleton	62746
288	The Percy	62747
292	The Southwold	62748
297	The Cottesmore	62749
298	The Pytchley	62750
205	The Albrighton	62751
214	The Atherstone	62752
217	The Belvoir	62753
222	The Berkeley	62754
226	The Bilsdale	62755

Original No	Name	BR No
230	The Brocklesby	62756
238	The Burton	62757
258	The Cattistock	62758
274	The Craven	62759
279	The Cotswold	62760
353	The Derwent	62761
357	The Fernie	62762
359	The Fitzwilliam	62763
361	The Garth	62764
362	The Goathland	62765
363	The Grafton	62766
364	The Grove	62767
365[5]	The Morpeth	62768
366	The Oakley	62769
368	The Puckeridge	62770
370	The Rufford	62771
374	The Sinnington	62772
375	The South Durham	62773
376	The Staintondale	62774
377	The Tynedale	62775

[5] At the height of the anti-Gresley campaign by Edward Thompson, engine No 365 was rebuilt with two *inside* cylinders

4. Class 'P2' three-cylinder 2-8-2 express locos

No	Name
2001	Cock o' the North
2002	Earl Marischal
2003	Lord President
2004	Mons Meg
2005	Thane of Fife
2006	Wolf of Badenoch

These engines were rebuilt as 4-6-2s—and ruined—by Thompson

5. Class 'B17' 4-6-0s—the 'Sandringhams'

Original No	Name	BR No
2800	Sandringham	61600
2801	Holkham	61601
2802	Walsingham	61602
2803[6]	Framlingham	61603
2804	Elvedon	61604
2805	Lincolnshire Regiment	61605
2806	Audley End	61606
2807[6]	Blickling	61607
2808	Gunton	61608
2809	Quidenham	61609
2810	Honingham Hall	61610
2811	Raynham Hall	61611
2812	Houghton Hall	61612

Original No	Name	BR No
2813	Woodbastwick Hall	61613
2814[6]	Castle Hedingham	61614
2815	Culford Hall	61615
2816[6]	Falloden	61616
2817[6]	Ford Castle	61617
2818	Wynyard Park	61618
2819	Welbeck Abbey	61619
2820	Clumber	61620
2821	Hatfield House	61621
2822	Alnwick Castle	61622
2823	Lambton Castle	61623
2824	Lumley Castle	61624
2825	Raby Castle	61625
2826	Brancepeth Castle	61626
2827	Aske Hall	61627
2828	Harewood House	61628
2829	Naworth Castle	61629
2830	Tottenham Hotspur	61630
2831	Serlby Hall	61631
2832	Belvoir Castle	61632
2833[6]	Kimbolton Castle	61633
2834	Hinchingbrooke	61634
2835	Milton	61635
2836	Harlaxton Manor	61636
2837	Thorpe Hall	61637
2838	Melton Hall	61638
2839[6]	Norwich City	61639
2840	Somerleyton Hall	61640
2841	Gayton Hall	61641
2842	Kilverstone Hall	61642
2843	Champion Lodge	61643
2844[6]	Earlham Hall	61644
2845	The Suffolk Regiment	61645
2846	Gilwell Park	61646
2847	Helmingham Hall	61647
2848	Arsenal	61648
2849	Sheffield United	61649
2850	Grimsby Town	61650
2851	Derby County	61651
2852	Darlington	61652
2853	Huddersfield Town	61653
2854	Sunderland	61654
2855	Middlesbrough	61655
2856	Leeds United	61656
2857	Doncaster Rovers	61657
2858	The Essex Regiment	61658
2859	East Anglian (streamlined)	61659
2860	Hull City	61660
2861	Sheffield Wednesday	61661
2862	Manchester United	61662
2863	Everton	61663
2864	Liverpool	61664
2865	Leicester City	61665

203

Original No	Name	BR No
2866	Nottingham Forest	61666
2867	Bradford	61667
2868	Bradford City	61668
2869	Barnsley	61669
2870	City of London (streamlined)	61670
2871[6]	Royal Sovereign	61671
2872	West Ham United	61672

[6] Engines 2803, 2807, 2814, 2816, 2817, 2833, 2839, 2844 and 2871 were rebuilt by Thompson as class 'B2' with two outside cylinders, 20 in by 26 in

6. Class 'K2' 2-6-0 for West Highland line

Original No	Name	BR No
4674	Loch Arkaig	61764
4682	Loch Lochy	61772
4684	Loch Garry	61774
4685	Loch Treig	61775
4691	Loch Morar	61781
4692	Loch Eil	61782
4693	Loch Sheil	61783
4697	Loch Quoich	61787
4698	Loch Rannoch	61788
4699	Loch Laidon	61789
4700	Loch Lomond	61790
4701	Loch Laggan	61791
4704	Loch Oich	61794

7. Class 'K4' 2-6-0 for West Highland line

Original No	Name	BR No
3441	Loch Long	61993
3442	The Great Marquess	61994
3443	Cameron of Lochiel	61995
3444	Lord of the Isles	61996
3445[7]	MacCailin Mor	61997
3446	MacLeod of MacLeod	61998

[7] Engine No 3445 was rebuilt by Thompson with two outside cylinders as the prototype for the new 'K1' class of 2-6-0

8. Class 'V2' 2-6-2 mixed traffic

Original No	Name	BR No
4771	Green Arrow	60800
4780	The Snapper, The East Yorkshire Regiment, The Duke of York's Own	60809
4806	The Green Howard, Alexandra Princess of Wales's Own, Yorkshire Regiment	60835
4818	St Peter's School, York, AD 627	60847
4831	Durham School	60860
4843	King's Own Yorkshire Light Infantry	60872
4844	Coldstreamer	60873

9. Class 'V4' 2-6-2 mixed traffic

Original No	Name	BR No
3401	Bantam Cock	61700

Index